"*The Breath of God* is a beautiful book, visually and spiritually. As lovely as its artwork is, its rich mix of words and images takes us to the depths of something lovelier still, which many people call God, whose name is both known and unknown. This book moves as the human heart moves, between the seen and the unseen, and somehow embraces it all. Read this book meditatively, in the spirit with which it was written, and it will open your heart—to yourself, to others, and ultimately to the beauty behind this world of suffering and joy."

 —**Parker J. Palmer,** author of *The Courage to Teach, A Hidden Wholeness, Let Your Life Speak,* and *Healing the Heart of Democracy*

"This wise book reveals Julie Hliboki as a person of peace, of deep interfaith appreciation, of profound self-awareness, and a master teacher of sacred expression."

 —**Robert McDermott,** Professor, California Institute of Integral Studies and Editor of *The New Essential Steiner*

"*The Breath of God,* written and compiled by Julie Hliboki, is a devotional poetic reflection on the most beautiful Names of God, offered through the language of personal experience bringing words together with beautiful artistry creating devotional songs based on the Monotheistic tradition. Dr. Hliboki's poetic reflections bring the reader together with the seeking heart of the wayfarer, a heart that sees beauty in all that exists, experiences divine in every reflection, appreciates the bounty and richness that she has received from the generosity of the Being, yet expressed in a contemporary language for the modern reader."

 —**Nahid Angha, Ph.D.,** Co-director of the International Association of Sufism and Executive Director of *Sufism Journal*

"A springboard to dive deep into the well of contemplative practice...each mandala an island on which to surface and rest for reflection and creative expression."

 —**Dr. Mary Pilat,** Purdue University

"As a teacher of contemplative practice, I am constantly reminded that most practices focus on only one dimension of experience—for example, the use of images rather than words. But Julie Hliboki moves past this narrowness, inviting us into a multi-dimensional contemplative experience. She draws on the wisdom of the Abrahamic spiritual paths to weave together processes of vocal, musical, and visual expression, as well as insights from the sacred words, texts, and sages. By allowing us to activate this full range of contemplative capacities, *The Breath of God* offers us a rare and much-needed experience: a profoundly integrated contemplative practice for the cultivation of a profoundly integrated life."

 —**Andrew Dreitcer, Ph.D.,** Associate Professor of Spirituality and Director of the Center for Engaged Compassion, Claremont School of Theology

"Julie Hliboki is an amazing person, a true entrepreneur of the Spirit. In this book she opens the door to an authentic interfaith pathway. For those new to this journey, she provides guidance for first steps on the contemplative journey."

—**Dr. Ben Campbell Johnson,** author of *Companions in Contemplation: Reflections on the Contemplative Path, Beyond 9/11: Christians and Muslims Together,* and *Hearing God's Call*

"A stunning feast of the spirit, this book describes a pathway to God. Through stories of her personal journey, the author shows us how we can breathe God too. By drawing upon faith traditions, she shares wisdom of the ancients. We have been invited on the journey, accompanied every step of the way."

—**Frances Henry,** founder of Global Violence Prevention

"Here is a contemporary and inspired presentation of the Names of God. They are presented in various creative modalities to inspire the reader in his/her own spiritual journey in the world. These are the beautiful divine names that will enlighten the seeker."

—**Aziza Scott,** head of the Esoteric School, Sufi Order International

"This book provides a way for people to find rest and peace in the midst of an often hectic life and to connect deep within to their own source of love and truth. The questions and contemplative expressions encourage a deep search for the sacred within."

—**Christina Puchalski, MD,** Director and Founder, The George Washington Institute for Spirituality and Health

"The author emphasizes her readers' capacity to embark on spiritual adventures of their own. One of her mandalas might prompt one to say, 'That's not how I perceive that concept.' I am sure that Hliboki's answer would be to hand each such person a brush of their own and a palette of paints."

—**Alexander Patico,** Secretary (North America), Orthodox Peace Fellowship

The Breath of God:

Thirty-Three Invitations to Embody Holy Wisdom

Julie Carlson Hliboki

Transilient Publishing

To all of you
who believe that sacred expression
can foster self-awareness
interfaith appreciation
and peace.
May we begin by
sharing our creativity
deepening our connections
and intentionally engaging in community.

Acknowledgments

I consider myself one of the most fortunate people on the planet. I see God everywhere—in friends and family, in flora and fauna, in animal companions and wildlife, in sunshine and stars, and in strangers and fellow travelers yet unknown. The Divine infiltrates every part of my life and resides in all that I experience. I witness God's fingerprints in the crafting of my days, the opening of my heart, and in this project for which I have such passion.

Many people have contributed their love, attention, and wisdom to the Ninety-Nine Names Peace Project. I have had the privilege of interacting with individuals from all walks of life while on this journey—persons of various faiths, ancestries, ethnicities, ages, cultures, and views. I am moved by their dedication to peaceful communities and their willingness to embrace me and take this project into their fold. We each recognize that we are in this together, but the networking and support extend beyond collaboration. They reach into love, that ingredient absolutely essential for peace to thrive. I am grateful to all who have touched me deeply. The world is a better place because of you, your dedication, and your contributions.

In particular, I wish to thank Dr. Ben Campbell Johnson for encouraging me to embrace God's leading. It was a conversation with Ben that ensured my diving headlong into this project. He assured me that the persistence with which this idea followed me for five years was a sure sign of the Divine's call. In my times of uncertainty, I think of Ben.

I extend a special thanks to those who contributed their efforts to creating this book. Amy Ferguson and Kathy Jennings provided thoughtful, skilled editing and insights as I attempted to express myself clearly. Karin Kinsey designed the beautiful graphics and page layout. Dave Hill of River Run Press scanned the mandalas into an electronic format and color-corrected the pieces to ensure visual accuracy as our medium shifted from watercolor paper to four-color printing. Countless others reviewed the work and offered words of encouragement to help move the project along.

Finally, I wish to thank my two beloveds—David and Maya. David is the love of my life, and our relationship makes my heart sing with joy. Every day I thank the Divine for this wonderful gift of love. I have learned so much with David about giving and receiving, opening and sharing, risking and flying. He loves and supports me for who I am and for that I am deeply blessed.

Maya is my fluffy, wonderful, funny canine companion elkhound who passed away as I finalized this book. I am grateful that she was willing to share of herself so fully and I delighted in the unending surprises of transformation, peace, and tranquility that she revealed on a daily basis. Maya believed strongly in the pack (her version of community) and could often be found lying under my desk with her paw forming the connection between the two of us. I miss her enormously.

Table of Contents

Part Three - Interfaith Appreciation

Introduction

The ministry that the Divine has blessed me with involves invitation, creativity, and community. For the past thirty years I have been co-creating environments with God that invite people to discover themselves, both personally and professionally. I have witnessed hundreds of breakthroughs, watching light bulbs ignite as illusions are released and the divine Self is birthed. Hearts are opened by God's hand, reaching into the depths of the soul, taking hold, and forming a new path.

My life's work is dedicated to helping people transform. I connect with people through my professional coaching, organizational development practice, teaching expressive arts graduate courses at a local university, leading transformative workshops and retreats, and directing the Ninety-Nine Names Peace Project. Through all of these, I view myself as an ambassador, extending invitations to connect with the Divine and embody love and compassion.

Religious and wisdom traditions teach us that contemplative practice can provide a powerful pathway to awareness, compassion, love, and oneness. Centering prayer, meditation, mindfulness, and *lectio divina* are just a few of the contemplative practices embraced by mainstream traditions. Contemplative practice opens our hearts to new forms of wakefulness and responsiveness. Engaging in expressive arts can provide a similar pathway to greater attentiveness and consciousness.

"Contemplative expression" is a term I have coined to help define the practice of accessing and sharing the Divine through mindful, reflective artistic endeavors. It combines contemplative practices with expressive arts to embody, reflect on, and creatively articulate our union with the Divine.

Through contemplative expression, we can engage in practices such as mindfulness, meditation, divination, and prayer to open to God's leading. We may then employ expressive arts—such as painting, drawing, writing poetry and prose, dance, movement, music, and drama—to illustrate and share our experiences. Contemplative expression reveals how God speaks to us, how God moves through us creatively. It allows us to embody this experience and offer our creative gifts back to God. It is a pathway to deepen our connection with the Divine, each other, our communities, and nature.

Contemplative practice and expressive arts can serve as a pathway to interfaith appreciation and peace. This approach brings to the interfaith and peacebuilding processes a pathway that circumvents the cognitive and allows one to express oneself through creativity rather than typical spoken communication. My experience shows that contemplative expression moves one directly to the heart and that one must open the heart for true healing to occur. Expressing ourselves through creative endeavors allows us to share what, at times, cannot be meaningfully conveyed with words.

The Breath of God is a product of my own practice of contemplative expression. It contains thirty-three invitations based on thirty-three of the Ninety-Nine Names of God, those characteristics by which Muslims regard

God. These names are attributes of God. The names come from the Qur'an, the Islamic holy book. Some of the same attributes of God, such as compassion, mercy, and guidance, are also found within the Bible and other sacred texts.

Contemplative expression can supplement much of the deep, consequential work undertaken by others in the interfaith and peacebuilding fields. To all of you who work toward interfaith appreciation and peace—in yourself, in your communities, and throughout the world—I hope that this book and its practices will support you.

Working with this Book

This book is an invitation. It is intended to be a devotional, a pathway to engaging with God. The mandalas for each of the thirty-three names included in this volume (the first volume of three) are based on visions that I received from the Divine. The mandalas and their corresponding text come to me one at a time, on God's time, through my own contemplative practice.

This book is also a work of contemplative expression. Part One describes my walk with God and how this work was born, as well as my contemplative expression process in painting the Names of God. Part Two encompasses the thirty-three Names of God with their respective contemplative expression elements:

- a mandala representing a characteristic of the Divine,
- a verse from the Qur'an and from the New and Old Testaments,
- an inspirational essay, song, or poem related to the characteristic,
- questions for reflection, and
- an invitation to engage creativity through expressive arts.

Part Three summarizes my Abrahamic interfaith immersion experience, offers a brief discussion about the value of interfaith appreciation, and invites readers to participate in the Ninety-Nine Names Peace Project.

I have painted all of the mandalas, posed the questions, and created the expressive arts engagements. I have also composed most of the essays, songs, poems, and prayers. Those writings that are not mine are attributed to their authors. For the verses, there were sometimes hundreds of possibilities from which to choose within the Qur'an and the Bible. For example, each surah (chapter) of the Qur'an begins with a reference to the Beneficent or Compassionate (Ar-Rahman) and the Merciful (Ar-Rahim). I developed a method for narrowing which verses to use, which I explain at the end of this book, and ultimately I chose those verses that spoke to me deeply. They represent one selection among many options. I invite you to engage with the Qur'an and the Bible to discover which verses speak to you.

Each person who interacts with this book will have an opportunity to learn from the Abrahamic faiths. You may discover there are more similarities than differences. This devotional is also a gateway to begin an interfaith gathering within your own community, engage with this book, and learn from each other. Perhaps you will create sacred art together or form a poetry group to express your faith. (You can find more information about The Ninety-Nine Names Peace Project in Part Three of this book.)

You are invited to creatively respond to the attributes to which the Names of God refer. For example, one of the Ninety-Names of God is Al-Musawwir, The Shaper of Beauty. Al-Musawwir is not a separate god but rather an attribute or characteristic of God as defined in the Qur'an, *the* one and only God. If our creative expression involves painting, we would not be painting Al-Musawwir. Rather, we would paint beauty—the characteristic arising from The Shaper of Beauty named Al-Musawwir in the Qur'an. For Al-Adl, The Utterly Just, we might write poetry about justice—the characteristic arising from The Utterly Just. For Ar-Rahim we might interpret, through dance, mercy—the characteristic arising from The Most Merciful. For An-Nur, light, and so on. In responding artistically to the characteristic to which the Names of God refer, we honor the Islamic tradition to refrain from creating an image of God. By sharing experiences of God through these creative endeavors we can move into a realm of peace with ourselves, each other, nature, and the Divine.

Interacting with the Mandalas Through Toning

One way you are invited to interact with a Ninety-Nine Names mandala is through toning. Toning refers to producing a sustained pitch with your voice, either by humming or by holding short (not long) vowel sounds. The tone may be so quiet as to be imperceptible to anyone other than you or it may be louder. Such a sound creates a vibration that, on the physiological level, releases tension and encourages relaxation. It can draw your awareness deep within your body, providing an opportunity for sensing your essence, perceiving a spiritual oneness, and opening to healing.

As you look at a mandala, such as As-Salam (peace), As-Sabur (patience), or Al- Musawwir (beauty) for example, you may hum or sing a short vowel sound—pronounced AH (as in far), EH (as in end), EE (as in see), OH (as in own), or OU (as in you). For As-Salam, tone the "a" vowels—AH AH. For As-Sabur, tone the "a" and "u" vowels—AH OU. For Al-Musawwir, tone the "u," "a," and "i" vowels—OU, AH, EE. As you tone with each of these different mandalas, note whether and where you feel a resonance in your body. Do your hands tingle? Does your chest or head vibrate? Try toning with several additional images to learn whether you perceive different results.

You may also try toning the name itself or select two names: one to tone as you inhale, the other to tone when you exhale. When toning the names, use "Ya" (meaning O, as in to call someone) in front of the name rather than "Al," "Ar," "At," "An," or "As." One of my favorite pairs is Ya-Rahman (O Compassion) on the in-breath and Ya-Hakim (O Wisdom) on the out-breath. This meditative practice of compassion and wisdom coincides for me with the Zen notion of "soft front" and "strong back."

Part One
The Breath of God

The following is an account of my walk with the Divine during the last ten years. It describes how these mandalas, the Ninety-Nine Names Peace Project, and this book were born. I share this personal account with the hope that those of you who have experienced similar phenomena may begin to appreciate just how common mystical experiences are. I believe we experience the mystical every day, but we are too busy to realize it. The breath of God is flowing constantly, inviting us into its presence. This requires our willingness to slow down, breathe, and feel what is occurring in the moment. When we are able to accomplish this simple task, we can more readily experience the mystical.

My Walk with the Divine

In January of 2000, I began to investigate healing through sound and vibration. Through a series of private lessons, I learned the practice of toning, a process by which a person emits a sustained single musical note on a pitch of his or her choosing. This meditative practice creates a vibrational resonance within one's body.

As an initiate, I delighted in the visceral access to my essence, the core of who I am, that toning gave me. Whenever I toned, I felt completely aligned physically, mentally, emotionally, and spiritually. I now realize that toning is one way for me, both as a transmitter and receiver, to communicate with the Divine. The physical sensation of this practice alerts me to God's presence within me.

The revelations I received early on through toning were extraordinary, mystical, and God-centered. During one of my early experiences I "saw" sound waves as wisps of smoke moving toward me. Angelic beings perched on these waves carried messages. As the waves drew near, a space of vibrational energy opened in my body close to my heart *chakra*, and the messages entered me, each one traveling to a different body part.

Chakra is a Sanskrit word that translates as "turning." It refers to wheel-like vortices which, according to traditional Indian medicine, are believed to be focal points of energy that allow for the reception and transmission of energies. The most well-known system in the West is that of seven chakras beginning at the base of the spine and moving up the body to the top of the head – root chakra, sacral chakra, solar plexus chakra, heart chakra, throat chakra, brow chakra, and crown chakra.

I noticed that when any part of my body received a message, the tension in that location released. As I concluded the toning practice I felt relaxed, refreshed, and physically energized, ready to face the day with renewed vigor. Shoulder knots, neck tension, and leg aches vanished, leaving me with a sense of completeness, grounded in the present moment and aware of the sanctity of life. This was my first direct experience of personal healing through sound vibration—where pathways opened to the Divine to realign wholeness.

In a later toning session, I experimented with sensing the vibrational patterns of colors. I wanted to know whether the qualities of individual colors might register in my mind and body. I worked with ten pieces of colored paper in six-inch squares—red, orange, yellow, green, blue, purple, pink, black, brown, and white. I began the experiment by selecting a color, closing my eyes, and sensing the characteristic of that particular color. I held my hand an inch above the paper and opened myself to feeling its attributes. To my surprise, each color presented a unique vibrational pattern signature. Each revealed its own temperature and texture. Even more intriguing was that on opening my eyes, I would "see" an embossed image of a body part embedded in the color. I carefully noted the results in my journal, later wondering about the potential healing relationship between the colors and the body parts.

Blindfolded, I then tested my ability to discern the paper's color based on sensing its vibration. I shuffled the squares, selected one, held my hand over it, and waited. Some of the colors I discerned immediately and correctly, others I could only guess. Interestingly, the colors that were easiest for me to distinguish were colors I tend to wear. I noted my attraction to these colors and how I felt physically when I wore them. Pink was soothing, blue grounding, red energizing, purple expanding. I was also able to sense several other colors—green, brown, and yellow—and noted that although these were not colors that I tended to wear, I was deeply drawn to them in nature. Green felt enlivening, brown rooted, and yellow warming. I did not receive any input from orange, black, or white.

Over the next two years I continued my studies in vibrational toning and sound healing, deepening my daily practice of meditative toning and experiencing mystical episodes. I attribute my healthy body and clear mind to my daily walks in nature. I did nearly all of my toning on these walks. One of my most memorable incidents occurred in the woods while I was walking my longtime canine companion, Veggie Boy.

It was late April on a bright and sunny afternoon and we meandered through the middle of a two-hundred acre preserve in the midst of a dale populated by dogwoods in full bloom. As Veggie and I crossed the center of the basin, I realized that I was listening to the most exquisite music I had ever heard. It sounded as if a symphony of seraphs was expressing their most intimate, creative nature. The resonance permeated me entirely. I looked for the source of the sound, a bit bewildered since we were far from any neighbors or sources of electricity. I stood in silence, listening closely, trying to follow the sound to its source.

A dogwood petal caught my eye, then another, then another. At once I knew that the sound was emanating from the thousands of dogwood petals in the glade, twinkling in the sunlight. Their beauty was breathtaking, and I yelled out, "Veggie, the dogwoods are singing to us!" For the next hour I sat in the glade listening to the petals sing and feeling their vibrational energy pour over me. It was as if I were being showered with love, laughter, and light.

The angelic energy radiated through my body, into and out of every pore, healing and aligning each cell. I felt God's presence everywhere and a profound union with all life. The world was lit with bright light as far as I could see, and then suddenly the music ceased. After a few deep breaths, I arose, feeling sated with love. I woke Veggie, who was sleeping under the pine trees, and headed for home.

A few weeks later, I was again traversing the woods, toning as I went, and was taken aback by a vision of a sphere filled with colorful geometric patterns. It was head-high and floating about four feet in front of me. As I stared at it, the colors twinkled and vibrated, just as the dogwood flowers had. I tried toning various sounds, and as my pitch changed so did the circle's patterns and colors. I was in awe of this spherical kaleidoscope that responded to changing vibrational tones from my body. As I played with toning and the responding imagery, I heard a voice inside me telling me that this was a healing mandala and I was to share it with the world. I sensed the voice was from God. The image vanished and I finished my walk contemplating how I might accept this invitation.

Once home, I looked up the word mandala in the dictionary and searched for images online. I delighted in discovering that mandala comes from the Sanskrit word for circle. The mandala represents wholeness and may be viewed as a model for the organizational structure of life itself—a cosmic diagram that reminds us of our relationship to the infinite, the world that extends both beyond and within our bodies and minds. Traditionally, mandalas incorporate symmetry and geometric patterns, often rosettes. Mandalas of the natural world might include spider webs, the petals of a rose, or a spiral galaxy.

My visions of mandalas continued through the next several days, and I felt compelled to capture them on paper. Not having any formal artistic training, I was at a loss as to where to begin. I tried drawing the images with colored pens, magic markers, and crayons, but the results seemed to lack the energy present in the visions. I sensed the medium needed to be more organic and contacted a friend who was a watercolor artist to borrow some of her materials.

The next day I sat down with watercolor paper and water-soluble crayons, intending to capture one of the healing mandalas on paper. I began toning and relaxed into a receptive state. My arms and hands began tingling, and I felt a wave of energy pass through my body beginning near my heart and flowing through my fingertips. I gathered plates, saucers, glasses, circular dinnerware of any size and, tracing them, drew the mandala. Sitting with the pencil outline of geometric patterns, I picked up my paintbrush, dipped it in water, and looked at the tin of crayons. One caught my eye because it appeared brighter than the others. I picked it up, brushed my paintbrush across its tip to collect color, and looked at the paper. My hand went to a particular section of the mandala, applied the paint, and the vision began to unfold. The process completely bypassed my intellect as if my hands knew exactly what to do.

I remained in this state for hours, losing all sense of time and space, absorbed in an energetic dance with God, inviting the Divine to flow through my body, out my fingertips, and onto paper. I felt God's healing presence enliven me. I sensed that this mandala captured and stored a healing, energetic property, similar to a photograph capturing and storing an image of light.

From the very start, I understood my part in painting these mandalas as one of co-creator and I found the process wonderfully healing. While painting I felt an absolute alignment with God's presence, utterly connected in every aspect of my being. The Holy Spirit danced through my body, and for the next two years I co-created nearly fifty healing mandalas. I was content to finish them, one by one, and placed them in a drawer in my studio. Periodically I would feel called to select one, tone with it, and receive its healing energy.

One day I felt inspired to arrange the entire collection on my floor, and in the midst of this display, a friend stopped by unexpectedly. Up until this point, I had not shared the mandalas with anyone because the experience of creating them was so personal for me.

This particular friend happened to be the art curator for a local hospital. When she saw the work she commented on the beauty, color, and energy of each piece and asked if I would allow her to exhibit the mandalas at the hospital. After I got past my initial shyness about having the art seen by others, we devised an exhibit that would display twenty-six select pieces and invite viewers to tone with the work so that they might perceive the art's energetic healing properties.

The opening of the *Healing Mandalas and Vibrational Imagery* exhibit was crowded with friends, art lovers, and patrons curious about vibrational energy. People toned with the mandalas and shared their experiences with each other. One experience I'll never forget came from a woman who approached me with apprehension and said, "I need to know what's going on here." After some probing on my part as to what she wanted to know, she revealed that she suffered from severe migraines and almost did not attend the exhibit that evening due to the pain she was experiencing. At the show, she decided to try toning, and while working with one of the mandalas, her migraine abated. She asked me for an explanation. We walked through several possibilities ranging from co-incidence to possibly the mandala's energetic healing properties affecting her body's chemistry. Regardless, I told her, I was happy she was feeling better.

About a year later, I was attending a silent Sufi retreat. While walking a labyrinth on a sunny day and toning one of the Ninety-Nine Names of God—Nur or light—a beautiful spherical image appeared. The energetic properties of this vision differed from my usual mandala experience. There was a deeper quality that moved beyond healing, so I stopped walking to sit with the sensations I was feeling in my body. When I closed my eyes, I saw an exhibit of peace-themed art. The exhibit was in a foreign country, and patrons came from various religions with a common interest in sharing peace-centered communities. Throngs of individuals milled about sharing their appreciation of art and initiating conversations about peace. They were drawn by the artwork but remained for the conversations. I heard God's voice utter that I was to create and exhibit the Ninety-Nine Names of God.

That evening I approached the Sufi retreat leader who also directs the Esoteric School of the Sufi Order International. I spoke with her about the vision, explaining that I felt inadequate to undertake such a project since

I knew so little about Sufism, Muslim traditions, and the Ninety-Nine Names. She invited me to pray with her. On concluding our prayer, she provided encouragement and permission to work with the Ninety-Nine Names. Later that night I spoke with the Divine about my reluctance to take on the project and confirmed that I was rejecting the calling. I felt something shut down in my body. For the next four years the call persisted, though I continued to reject it. During this time, I did not experience any visions of healing mandalas.

In 2008, I had the privilege of being introduced to Ben Campbell Johnson's writing on discernment, knowing God, and his personal journey. In his book *Hearing God's Call*, a single line drew my attention, "A call from God persists." I realized that the one constant force in my life through the past eight years had been the Ninety-Nine Names project. I was perplexed. Could it be that the Divine was still inviting me to realize my vision? Is that what God wanted for my life? The project still seemed too complex and yet perhaps, in my desire to be led into God's desire for me, I was ready to trust the call. Questions flooded my mind.

Through prayer, discernment, and the encouragement of loved ones, I have since waded deeply into this process. This is my co-creative dance with the Divine. My willingness to be led through discerning God's will provides me with a sense of excitement, peace, and inspiration. I am grateful that I feel the Holy Spirit resonate in my body, that God speaks to me on waves of sound, and that I have been granted a calling that combines contemplation, art, and peace.

Each of us hears the Divine in our own way, and accesses holy wisdom through our own path. I invite you to join me on this wondrous journey and to deepen your discovery.

My Process of Painting the Names

Painting is a sacred practice for me, filled with God's love and grace. I have come to understand that this is my process, the process that is true for me, and I realize that others may experience something completely different in their creative endeavors. All of my paintings have been created with the spirit of the Divine inspiring me. I have tremendous gratitude for these creative gifts and visions and accept them with humility. Whatever you experience on your journey with sacred practice is worth celebrating and I encourage you to share your creative insights and expressions with others.

When settling in to paint one of the Ninety-Nine Names I often feel a particular physical sensation I have come to know as God preparing to send a vision. When this occurs, whether day or night, I begin to pray and meditate and turn to S. al-Halveti's *The Most Beautiful Names* to usher in the vision.

I hold the book in my hands and patiently wait in prayer until I feel moved to open the book at a particular place. Each page within the book portrays a different name. I do not know which name I am being asked to paint until I open the book to discover where the Divine has led me.

When I read the name that has been revealed and the page-long description of that attribute, a visual image of the name in the style of a mandala begins to appear. By creating an internal environment of openness, expansiveness, and receptivity in my body, I hold the space for the vision to fully materialize. The revelation of the mandala may take shape in seconds or gradually over a longer period. While the vision is developing, a physical vibration activates at the base of my skull and courses down my arms to my fingertips. It is energizing like an electrical current, yet is soft, gentle, and full, like water flowing gently in a stream. Centering myself in prayer, this current spills out of my hands onto the paper and I begin sketching the mandala.

I work with water-soluble pastels, pencils, and crayons arranged in tins and grouped by color. Often when I apply paint to a portion of a mandala, a color will either emanate from the paper or will appear brighter in the tins than the other colors, calling to me. Sometimes a color will visually vibrate in a tin. Other times I will hear an internal voice suggesting a color for a particular area. With a paintbrush I lift the pigment from the pastel, pencil, or crayon. I find this a delicate, meditative application that encourages patience, care, and listening at each step of the painting practice.

In painting the Ninety-Nine Names of God, I have a deep sense of awe and reverence for both the process of painting and for each created image. I pray that in sharing this process and journey, I will honor, express, and impart the love and beauty of the Divine. My hope is that anyone who does not experience this work in the same way might offer me grace and compassion for my intent.

Part Two
Embodying Holy Wisdom

Compassion
(Ar-Rahman)

Anyway

People are often unreasonable, irrational, and self-centered.
Forgive them anyway.

If you are kind, people may accuse you of selfish, ulterior motives.
Be kind anyway.

If you are successful, you will win some unfaithful friends and some genuine
enemies. Succeed anyway.

If you are honest and sincere, people may deceive you.
Be honest and sincere anyway.

What you spend years creating, others could destroy overnight.
Create anyway.

If you find serenity and happiness, some may be jealous.
Be happy anyway.

The good you do today will often be forgotten.
Do good anyway.

Give the best you have, and it will never be enough.
Give your best anyway.

In the final analysis, it is between you and God.
It was never between you and them anyway.

—Attributed to Mother Teresa

Insights About Compassion from the Abrahamic Faiths

Islam
And make yourself submissively gentle to them with compassion, and say: O my Lord! have compassion on them, as they brought me up [when I was] little.
Qur'an, 17.24

Christianity
As Jesus went ashore he saw a great throng, and he had compassion on them, because they were like sheep without a shepherd; and he began to teach them many things.
Mark 6:34

Judaism
The Lord is good to all, and his compassion is over all that he has made. All thy works shall give thanks to thee, O Lord, and all thy saints shall bless thee!
Psalms 145:9-10

An Invitation into Contemplative Expression…

With art materials and a journal in hand, find a quiet place to sit. Close your eyes and take several deep, centering breaths. Allow an image to come to mind that represents self-doubt. Open your eyes and draw this image and write a few paragraphs describing it and the effect of self-doubt in your life. Close your eyes again and take several deep, centering breaths. As you inhale, invite the feeling of compassion to wash over you, rinsing away the self-doubt you illustrated moments ago. Take several breaths, inhaling compassion and exhaling self-doubt. Open your eyes and draw yourself steeped in self-compassion. Notice the differences between the two images and write about those in your journal.

Mercy
(Ar-Rahim)

A Shift in Mercy

For months I have been contemplating the notion of mercy, or more precisely the phrase, "at the mercy of." Lately, it seems that all of the choices I need to make are taking longer than I believe they should. I've been behaving as if these decisions depend on the decisions of others. I've felt at the mercy of others' schedules, whims, and ambivalence.

Unfortunately, feeling "at the mercy of" due to emotionally triggered events—those situations that stimulate our core fears and activate survival skills—generates a fight-or-flight response in us, as if the incident were a matter of life or death. At some point during our past, a similar incident probably was life-or-death and evoked deep fear. As infants and small children, we were at risk of death if our caretakers withdrew their care. We later developed defenses to protect ourselves and skills that attempted to predict and control our surroundings. Our goal was to avoid being "at the mercy of."

As adults, we learn to respond to triggers in alternate ways and to view events through lenses other than our childhood traumas. We also discover that circumstances that feel like life-or-death are in reality not so. We survive losing jobs, relationships, loved ones, physical abilities, financial stability, and status. Given enough time to heal and make new choices, many of us thrive in our new situations. Yes, someone or something may have influenced the course of our life, perhaps before we were ready, but they did not control our response to that change. Even facing death, we can choose our response.

There is a wonderful story my beloved shared with me that illustrates this beautifully. A monk had been captured and imprisoned for practicing his religion. Determined to continue his daily meditations undisturbed, he barred the door to his cell. When the prison guard discovered this during his rounds, he pounded on the cell door with his gun, demanding that the monk open the door. The monk continued meditating in prayer, ignoring the guard. Enraged, the guard pounded harder, shouting at the monk to open the door or he would kill him. The monk continued his prayers and meditations, ignoring the guard. Further enraged, the guard left and returned with a battering ram and knocked the door down. Entering the cell with his gun aimed, he looked at the monk, and shouted, "What's wrong with you! Don't you know I have the power to kill you?" The monk responded simply, "Don't you know that I have the power to let you?" With that the guard begged forgiveness and let the monk go.

Mercy

In this story, the guard clearly held the means to kill the monk, but he did not have the power to control the monk. The monk could not predict the future. Even if he had opened the door, the guard might have killed him. The monk was prepared to live or die, trusting that the one authentic act he could do was continue to meditate in prayer. The rest was left to the unfolding of life. The monk was never "at the mercy of" the guard.

How often are we willing to respond to situations authentically regardless of the outcome? Are there ways we can shape our response in an attempt to influence what we perceive is an uncontrollable outcome? Are we willing to be patient and sit with something until we can sense a direction…and if no direction is revealed, accept ambiguity for the time being?

In Western society, we are rewarded for knowing and shamed for not knowing. We are rewarded for "planning our work and working our plan" as though this can guarantee a positive, calculated outcome. We have no idea what life will deliver at any given moment, and this creates fear. We widely accept the expectation that we should know or appear to know everything, as if by agreeing to this, we can defeat the unpredictability of life and be less afraid.

Our fear of being "at the mercy of" wreaks havoc in relationships when we form expectations, manipulate situations, attempt to control, forecast outcomes, and shame others and ourselves. Consequently, we mask our authentic selves, our deeply felt responses, and our innate sense to respond helpfully to any situation. Might we choose instead to be present and grateful for all that God is bestowing on us and trust that life will be OK regardless of the outcome?

Recently, my concept of mercy began to transform. First, I received an e-mail passage from Joan Chittister entitled "What Is Advent All About?" from *The Liturgical Year.* She speaks of slowing down and learning to wait in the dark, cold, unknowing; we become who we are as we stay present, receive God's signs, and give up our self—our need to know, predict, control, and consume. Only then can we recognize where God's grace and mercy is leading us in every moment.

In several situations in my life right now, time seems suspended. I feel a need to make a decision within a specific timeframe, but instead, the appropriate timeline appears to be "not yet." In granting these situations more time and space, I am becoming clearer about my needs and less attached to a particular outcome. For example, recently I was meeting with a new friend, discussing two options for teaching a course at the local university. I noticed myself uttering internally, "I trust God to lead me in the right direction, and whatever decision is made, I will follow that in faith." Any inclination to a certain outcome was absent. I did not register one preference over another between the two choices. I was unable to determine which choice was better as both had pros and cons. My propensity to predict vanished, and I grasped that controlling the outcome was unnecessary. Instead, I expressed myself as clearly and authentically as possible, stated my desires, and invited collaboration in the decision-making. I created space for healthy possibilities to emerge and encouraged patience and time to realize a decision.

In learning to wait patiently, I've discovered that decisions come in their own time. The more I honor this, the less attached I am to the outcome and the less I feel "at the mercy of." Non-attachment is different from being detached, where one might not care. I care deeply. However, I believe that whichever route I eventually choose will be fine—actually it will be great. I am acknowledging and honoring my desires, those co-created with God. In letting go, I am not attached to the form of how those desires will be met.

I am beginning to understand that when one places faith in God, one is never at the mercy of anyone or anything. Unquestionably, people can make decisions that affect my life, but they cannot control my response, my walk with God, or my trust that any circumstance can be turned toward the light.

The first time I painted Mercy I had a difficult time with it. Rather than the typical inspired flow, I felt tense. The shapes on the paper were angular, sharp, and controlled. Colors conflicted with each other, arguing for position and attention. As I painted, I felt increasingly tight, frustrated, and confused. The mandala was a jumble of edginess. In frustration, I dropped my paintbrush and left my studio for a long walk.

During the walk, my mind wandered, unraveling and softening what I had just experienced. About two miles into the trek, I realized that the painting was a reflection of my often feeling "at the mercy of." Unexpected psychic and physical pain flooded my body and suddenly dissipated. I felt purged, expansive, open, and light. This cellular cleansing released what seemed like decades of stored fear and pain tied to my encounters of those who I felt still exerted power over me. Their previous ability to hurt me was real, but my current ability to take care of myself through my choices and responses is also real.

I finished my walk and returned to my studio. I felt Mercy come over me in a new way, the mercy of compassion, care, kindness, and love. This second mandala flowed smoothly onto the watercolor paper. With it came the richness of humility and gratitude I've come to know so well from my encountering God.

Dear Loved Ones...

How might you respond to a situation authentically regardless of the outcome? In contrast, when do you control your response to achieve what you hope is a predictable outcome? Are you willing to be patient until you can sense a direction...and if no direction occurs, accept uncertainty for the time being? Where do you find and offer mercy?

An Invitation into Contemplative Expression...

With your art materials, find a comfortable place to sit, close your eyes, and breathe deeply. Reflect on a circumstance when you experienced a sense of being "at the mercy of." Notice who was involved, what you experienced, and where you still carry this in your body. Open your eyes and draw what this feels like in your body. Then, go for a walk outside. Allow the fresh air to cleanse any tension that you are holding in your body. As you walk, tone the blessings of humility and gratitude, sounding the vowels from these two words—"ou-ee-ee-ee-ah-ee-ou-eh." When you return, create a new drawing that expresses having mercy for those difficult people in your life.

Peace
(As-Salam)

Embracing Uncertainty, Entering Peace

There is a robin nesting in a poplar tree in my backyard outside my office window. I have been watching her for the past three weeks, first building her nest, then laying eggs, now hatching her young. On cool mornings, she fluffs her feathers, expanding herself to nearly three times her normal size in order to keep her young warm. On warmer days, she contracts her feathers, maintaining consistent temperature so that her young thrive. When she leaves the nest for food, she is not absent for more than a few seconds.

There are several grackles and cowbirds in the backyard trying to unseat her. I'm not sure whether they intend to steal her nest, kill the hatchlings, regain territory, or if they have some other motive. The first time I saw an invader approach the nest I cringed and thought "oh no, how do I stop this?" Yet every time, mama robin darts out of her nest, flies frantically toward the intruders, and chases them away. She is relentless. Her instinct to protect her young is so strong that she is willing to risk her life against the much larger birds.

Thus far her efforts have been successful, and her little ones are growing strong. The risk she takes to protect the nest produces a safe haven for the hatchlings. The moment-to-moment uncertainty continues about whether the young will reach a size where they can venture out on their own and care for themselves. Even so, whenever she is unseated, her instinctual response is to care for her babies. Love trumps uncertainty.

I experience this interplay between love and uncertainty in my own life and am aware of how a sense of perceived certainty can create a feeling of safety. The important term here is "perceived" since, in reality, certainty is an illusion. Intermingling certainty with safety often drives us to try to predict and control the future, each other, and our circumstances. We believe so strongly that certainty or predictability will make us safe and reduce our vulnerability that we trade our lives for the illusion of security. We remain in jobs that deplete our souls, stay in relationships that don't feed us, and immerse ourselves in busyness disguised as productivity.

What if, rather than focusing on certainty for our safety, we focused on Love, with a capital "L," Love from the source of all, the Divine? How would our lives transform if we opened our hearts and embraced uncertainty knowing that we are held closely in the hands of God? What if we pursued our passions as our vocation, entered into mutually loving primary relationships, slowed down enough to experience the wonders that surround us, and contributed to the world in our own unique ways? How might we enter into faith and trust more deeply in ourselves, each other, and the Divine?

As I've sat with this, I have had a number of insights about what it means to turn toward Love in all that I am. A key theme seems to be that the more boldly I walk toward Love, the safer I feel, and the safer I feel, the more boldly I can walk toward Love. With Love, I feel solid in my core, settled in mind and body, able to trust my ability to respond to and engage with whatever life brings me. It is not about certainty, it is about embracing all of life, fully entering into what Love provides and letting go of what I no longer need. This is, perhaps, the cycle of healing.

I am amazed by our capacity to give and receive Love and recognize the equal capacity to be open to and experience vulnerability. By continually turning toward Love in those times of vulnerability, I can provide myself and others the spaciousness, time, and support needed for healing. Yes, opening one's heart more deeply to Love is risky, and yes, letting go of illusions creates vulnerability, but uncertainty is the reality of life. Why not embrace it?

Dear Loved Ones...

What are the areas in your life that feel most uncertain? How might you embrace this uncertainty and enter the fullness of the experience? Who can you call on to help guide you to a place of peace? What practices will aid you in slowing down enough to sense the Divine's presence?

An Invitation into Contemplative Expression...

With art materials in hand, find a comfortable space where you can listen to music. Select several songs that evoke a sense of calm for you. As you listen to each selection, notice how your body is responding. Create an artistic expression illustrating the interplay between the music and your body's response.

A Prayer for Peace

Send Thy peace, O Lord,
which is perfect and everlasting, that our souls may radiate peace.

Send Thy peace, O Lord,
that we may think, act, and speak harmoniously.

Send Thy peace, O Lord,
that we may be contented and thankful for Thy bountiful gifts.

Send Thy peace, O Lord,
that amidst our worldly strife we may enjoy thy bliss.

Send Thy peace, O Lord,
that we may endure all, tolerate all in the thought of thy grace and mercy.

Send Thy peace, O Lord,
that our lives may become a divine vision,
and in Thy light all darkness may vanish.

Send Thy peace, O Lord,
our Father and Mother,
that we Thy children on earth may all unite in one family.

Amen.

—Prayer by Pir Hazrat Inayat Khan

Guardian
(Al-Muhaymin)

The Breath of God

Just a Closer Walk With Thee

Islam

*And We have revealed to you the
Book with the truth, verifying what
is before it of the Book and a guard-
ian over it, therefore judge between
them by what Allah has revealed,
and do not follow their low desires
to turn away from the truth
that has come to you....*
Qur'an, 5.48

Christianity

*I am the good shepherd; I know my
own and my own know me, as the
Father knows me and I know the
Father; and I lay down my life
for the sheep.*
John 10:14–15

Judaism

*Consider how I love thy precepts!
Preserve my life according to thy
steadfast love. The sum of thy word
is truth; and every one
of thy righteous ordinances
endures forever.*
Psalms 119:159–160

I am weak, but Thou art strong;
Jesus, keep me from all wrong;
I'll be satisfied as long
As I walk, let me walk close to Thee.

Just a closer walk with Thee,
Grant it, Jesus, is my plea,
Daily walking close to Thee,
Let it be, dear Lord, let it be.

Through this world of toil and snares,
If I falter, Lord, who cares?
Who with me my burden shares?
None but Thee, dear Lord, none but Thee.

When my feeble life is o'er,
Time for me will be no more;
Guide me gently, safely o'er
To Thy kingdom shore, to Thy shore.

—Traditional Folk Song

An Invitation into Contemplative Expression…

Find a favorite book of inspirational writings. It can be a sacred text, a book of poetry, a devotional, a song book…whatever speaks to you. Close your eyes, breathe deeply, and ask the Divine for clarity about an issue you have been struggling with, one for which you are seeking guidance. Sit for several minutes in this quiet state, holding your book in your hands. When you are ready, open the book to a random page and read what that page has to offer. Write about your seeking, the response, and what this means to you.

Self-Sufficiency
(Al-Aziz)

The Tiny Flame

Islam

Allah—surely nothing is hidden from Him in the earth or in the heaven. He it is Who shapes you in the wombs as He likes; there is no god but He, the Mighty, the Wise.
Qur'an, 3:5–6

Christianity

Your eye is the lamp of your body; when your eye is sound, your whole body is full of light; but when it is not sound, your body is full of darkness. Therefore be careful lest the light in you be darkness. If then your whole body is full of light, having no part dark, it will be wholly bright, as when a lamp with its rays gives you light.
Luke 11:34-36

Judaism

Behold, thou desirest truth in the inward being; therefore teach me wisdom in my secret heart.
Psalms 51:6

Sometimes the light inside me feels like a tiny flame that could easily be extinguished if not protected. This small flame, residing deep in the core of my belly, flickers to remind me of its presence. It persists, even when surrounded by darkness, emptiness, nothingness.

Sitting in meditation I recognize my desire to fan the flame, to illuminate the darkness, to see what is present. I desire to fill my core, my belly, my entire body with light.

How do I embolden this flame?

By creating space through relaxation, calming my mind, relinquishing expectations, being present…

By offering compassion for myself and others, recognizing that anyone at anytime can feel the fragility of their tiny flame…

By sensing kindness from my body, my beloved, my friends, my canine companion…

By embracing acts of love like wet dog kisses, holding my beloved's hand, exchanging greetings with neighbors, offering prayers, tending gardens, feeding birds, sharing a meal…

By entering the Divine presence, basking in the light that radiates through me and connects me to all other light in the universe…

These are just a handful of the intentional practices I engage in to mindfully kindle the tiny flame within me.

Ah, my flame is now strong, brilliant, ever expanding. Simply thinking about these intentions has the desired effect. I realize that, no matter how tiny my flame feels, this light does not require protection—it can never be extinguished. This is the true divine spark within me, within all of us. We are all divine light. How will you grow your flame?

Self-Sufficiency

Dear Loved Ones...

Where do you feel the divine spark in your body? What practices might you engage in to discover, nourish, and grow this flame? How might you share acts of love, both giving and receiving completely? How does this help you face the inevitability of your own death?

An Invitation into Contemplative Expression...

Sitting in a comfortable position with your eyes closed, imagine a tiny flame flickering inside your belly. Notice how the flame moves, as a candle might in a room with a slight breeze. With your breath, inhale and intentionally stoke the flame so that it increases slightly in size. With each inhalation fan the flame a bit more until it fills the cavity of your torso. Feel the warmth of this flame as it permeates your cells, organs, and tissues. Allow your body to sway with the flame as its light dances inside your being. Acknowledge that this light is the permanence of spirit, ever present, even through death.

Simple Gifts

'Tis the gift to be simple, 'tis the gift to be free,
'Tis the gift to come down where we ought to be,
And when we find ourselves in the place just right,
'Twill be in the valley of love and delight.

'Tis the gift to be loved and that love to return,
'Tis the gift to be taught and a richer gift to learn,
And when we expect of others what we try to live each day,
Then we'll all live together and we'll all learn to say,

When true simplicity is gained,
To bow and to bend we shan't be ashamed,
To turn, turn will be our delight,
Till by turning, turning we come round right.

Tis the gift to have friends and a true friend to be,
'Tis the gift to think of others not to only think of "me",
And when we hear what others really think and really feel,
Then we'll all live together with a love that is real.

—Shaker Folk Song

Compeller
(Al-Jabbar)

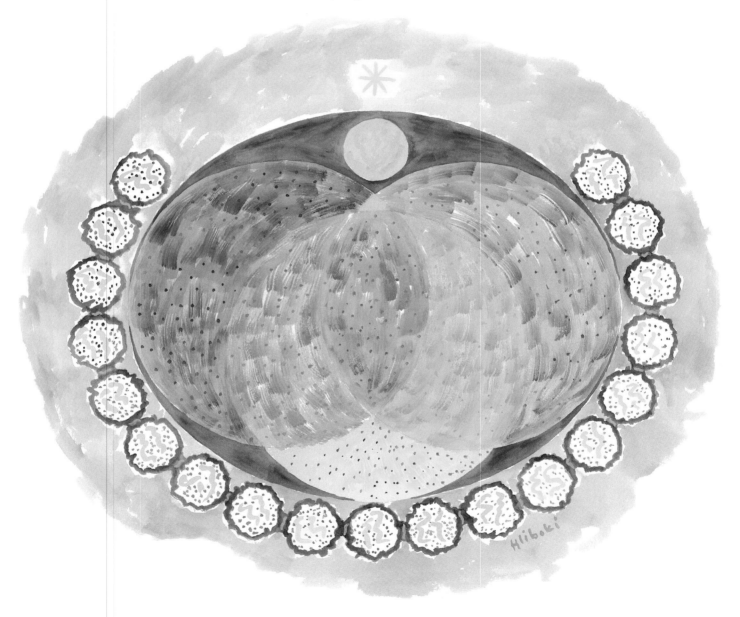

Reacting Versus Responding

As I consider the crisis in Haiti resulting from the earthquake of 2010, I've been deliberating on how I might contribute to the healing that is desperately needed on so many levels. I've noticed that there are two distinct sensations that I feel in my body about this question of contributing. One feels frantic; the other feels calm. The frantic sensation is *reacting*, driven by a *need* to make a difference. The calm sensation is *responding*, driven by a *desire* to make a difference. I hadn't realized there was such a distinction between these two pathways to action until I experienced them in direct proximity to each other.

When we witness a catastrophe as devastating as the crisis in Haiti, our first response is often one of shock and numbness. We can hardly find the words to describe what we are feeling, let alone how we might respond. If we are outsiders to the calamity, our focus may involve gathering data to intellectualize the circumstances, listening to newscasters frame the conditions, or simply tuning out what seems unbearable. If we are insiders, if the crisis has touched us personally, our response may also include participating directly in rescue efforts, forming communities that exchange the latest information, or carefully planning when we will engage firsthand to heal or repair the abounding brokenness.

Regardless of how we respond, the motivation behind our response speaks volumes about our current condition and our ability to authentically participate in sustainable healing. Are we responding to a calling, an invitation to act? Or are we reacting, through compulsion, to make a change we believe is necessary? Are we weighing our decisions with discernment? Are we asking what is required of us and responding accordingly? What discretionary measures are we enlisting to determine how we can be of service? Reacting and responding do not feel the same to me and, although I do both, I hope to react less and respond more by comprehending the motivation for each action more fully.

When I react, it is often compulsive. Dictionary.com defines compulsive as "a strong, usually irresistible impulse to perform an act, especially one that is irrational or contrary to one's will." When I respond, it is often because I feel called. Something is being drawn through me, stirring me to participate. Dictionary.com has numerous definitions for "call" and "called," including "an invitation to come" and "summoned as if by divine command."

Being Compelled

In my experience, reactionary, compulsive acts are motivated by a sense of scarcity, need, and a desire to fix. Responses made at my discretion focus on abundance, desire, supporting, and entering a persistent path. Discerning incorporates waiting and weighing wisdom rather than acting on a whim. With compulsion, my body feels scattered. I am head-based, frantic, and uneasy. In responding, my body operates from my core. I am heart-based, centered, and balanced. Most importantly, reacting seems to be tied to spoken or unspoken expectations, whereas responding invites creative solutions from a place of authenticity. When we are called into action, we are being asked to recognize the core of who we are and contribute to the wholeness of the situation from that place.

My favorite quote by Howard Thurman is, "Don't ask yourself what the world needs. Ask yourself what makes you come alive and then go do that. Because what the world needs are people who have come alive." What calls you? And how do you respond?

I feel a strong desire to respond to the crisis in Haiti. However I am fully aware that I am unclear what my response should be. I am praying, talking with those who can provide me guidance, loving those I know who are suffering, providing financial support, and praying more. I am working to discern, through prayer and meditation, what I might contribute and when is it needed. Patience is difficult at a time like this, but crucial. I'm certain my compulsion to hop on the next plane to Haiti to "help" would land me in the way of those who can actually make a difference right now. At some point, perhaps in a few months, being in Haiti will be useful. And yet, as I write these words, I feel physically agitated, compelled to spring into action and do something to address all of the suffering. It is heart wrenching to witness…so again I pray for guidance.

In painting Al-Jabbar, The Compeller, I am struck by how this characteristic of God accesses and blends the force of compulsion with the authenticity of responding to a call. The Compeller calls us boldly into action to contribute those gifts that we were blessed to share. In any situation, if we are patient and listen for wisdom, we will discover how to apply those gifts in a helpful and healing way. Our challenge is to resist the urge to react—on the one hand to control, manipulate, and force change or, on the other hand, to withdraw and avoid—from a place of compulsion. In a crisis, it is particularly difficult to resist that urge. Faith, trust, and prayer aid me in listening for the call.

Dear Loved Ones…

What triggers a reaction in you rather than a response? What measures are you enlisting to determine how you can be of service? How do you employ discernment to weigh your decisions? What calls to you and what is your response?

An Invitation into Contemplative Expression…

Gather a few art supplies and find a quiet place to sit. Close your eyes and breathe deeply. Recall a recent time when you felt called into action and you reacted from a place of compulsion. Open your eyes and draw an abstract image of your reaction. Next, for that same situation, consider what a response might have looked like, rather than a reaction. Draw an abstract image of your response. Compare the two drawings and write down words that express what you notice about the images.

And [Jesus] said to his disciples,
"Therefore I tell you, do not be anxious about your life,
what you shall eat, nor about your body, what you shall put on.
For life is more than food, and the body more than clothing.

Consider the ravens: they neither sow nor reap,
they have neither storehouse nor barn, and yet God feeds them.
Of how much more value are you than the birds!

And which of you by being anxious
can add a cubit to his span of life?
If then you are not able to do as small a thing as that,
why are you anxious about the rest?

Consider the lilies, how they grow;
they neither toil nor spin; yet I tell you,
even Solomon in all his glory was not arrayed like one of these.

But if God so clothes the grass which is alive in the field today
and tomorrow is thrown into the oven,
how much more will he clothe you, O men of little faith!

And do not seek what you are to eat and what you are to drink,
nor be of anxious mind.
For all the nations of the world seek these things;
and your Father knows that you need them.
Instead, seek his kingdom,
and these things shall be yours as well.

Fear not, little flock, for it is your Father's good pleasure
to give you the kingdom.
Sell your possessions, and give alms;
provide yourselves with purses that do not grow old,
with a treasure in the heavens that does not fail,
where no thief approaches and no moth destroys.

For where your treasure is, there will your heart be also."

–Luke 12:22–34

Beauty
(Al-Musawwir)

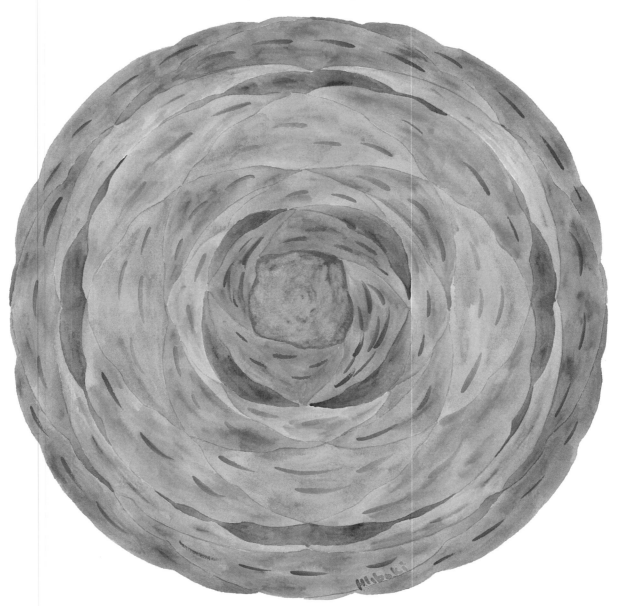

Beauty in the Midst of Cancer

I have a dear friend who is facing her third round of cancer. This time she is trying chemotherapy to defeat the persistent spread of unwanted cells. After her first treatment, clumps of her hair began falling out. Two weeks ago she chose to shave her head and, rather than purchase a wig, she is donning colorful, coordinated headscarves that attract attention to her skull.

One morning, when we were having tea and homemade cookies, she removed her pink floppy hat and bared her closely cropped hair, shaved almost to the surface. She looked exquisite, in a Sinead O'Connor kind of way. I told her she was beautiful. It wasn't just her appearance that beamed loveliness, it was her energy. She radiated light and goodness and courage and faith and joy and humor, all from a strong soul desiring life. To be in her company was to be in the presence of beauty.

I spent time with my friend both in nature and during her treatments. As we sauntered through the exploding fall colors in the woods near her home, her spirits carried both her body and the conversation along the paths of splendor. For the week prior, I had been meditating with Al-Musawwir, The Shaper of Beauty and wondering what would appear when I began to paint. As I hiked with my friend, I took in the fall colors, her multihued headscarf, and the vibrant blue sky. I pondered how these shades might influence my painting of Beauty. I subsequently let go of any expectation, trusting that Beauty would come to me as it wished to be revealed.

The evening that I painted Beauty I prayed for my friend, sending her healing energy and prayers of love. Slowly it sank into my bones that she has cancer—cancer—for the third time! I knew this, but the full impact hit me that night. I can only imagine what she is going through. My most difficult health issue is fluctuating hormone levels, which are uncomfortable but far from life-threatening.

Malformed cells are attempting to take over my friend's body. She is doing what she can to counteract this effect, to preserve her life, and she is accomplishing this with grace and love and gratitude and beauty. She radiates life and is a beacon for all to follow. I dedicate the peace-filled, healing energetic properties of this mandala, "Beauty" to her and all those struggling with cancer. Always remember just how extraordinarily beautiful you are.

Beauty

Dear Loved Ones...

Where do you find beauty? What does it mean to have a strong soul that desires life? How do you embrace those challenges that can, at times, drop us to our knees? Who in your life needs to be reminded about how beautiful they are?

An Invitation into Contemplative Expression...

With pen and paper in hand, find a quiet place to sit, preferably in nature. Close your eyes and take several deep breaths. As you inhale, acknowledge the beauty that is within you. As you exhale, honor the beauty that is around you. Breathe in this rhythm for several minutes, noticing the beauty within and without, the inner and the outer. Next, open your eyes and soak in the beauty that surrounds you, absorbing it into your very core. Allow a person to come to mind who could benefit from a reminder about their inner beauty. Write a poem or journal entry in honor of their beauty and how you witness their expression of it in the world.

O God of our salvation,
who art the hope of all the ends of the earth,
and of the farthest seas;
who by thy strength hast established the mountains,
being girded with might;
who dost still the roaring of the seas,
the roaring of their waves,
the tumult of the peoples;
so that those who dwell at earth's farthest bounds
are afraid at thy signs;
thou makest the outgoings of the morning and the evening
to shout for joy.

Thou visitest the earth and waterest it,
thou greatly enrichest it;
the river of God is full of water;
thou providest their grain,
for so thou hast prepared it.

Thou waterest its furrows abundantly,
settling its ridges,
softening it with showers,
and blessing its growth.

Thou crownest the year with thy bounty;
the tracks of thy chariot drip with fatness.

The pastures of the wilderness drip,
the hills gird themselves with joy,
the meadows clothe themselves with flocks,
the valleys deck themselves with grain,
they shout and sing together for joy.

—Psalms 65:5–13

Force
(Al-Qahhar)

The Breath of God

The Aftermath of Catastrophes

I have been contemplating the aftermath of the earthquake that hit Haiti, celebrating the small victories of rescue and feeling deep sorrow for the loss and devastation. This disaster is particularly close to my heart as my beloved spent nearly two decades of his career with the Centers for Disease Control working with the people of Haiti. A medical epidemiologist, his focus on neglected tropical diseases often placed him in the heart of Leogane, where so much destruction has occurred, where he worked so closely and developed so many heartfelt ties with the Haitian doctors and people he served.

I have noticed the pain in his eyes over the loss of dear friends, colleagues, and patients. Monitoring all varieties of news sources, David has shared with me each day what he learned about his friends, those he was able to reach and those he still has not heard from. His network of CDC friends established an instant community via e-mail, requesting any information about colleagues and their circumstances.

A commentator on National Public Radio said that this disaster was one of poverty, not natural forces. San Francisco has withstood earthquakes of more than 7.0 on the Richter scale in the past decade with little damage and loss of life. In Haiti, the same force earthquake has flattened miles, reducing structures to rubble and life to chaos. In such a fragile place, basic existence is ever more tenuous for millions of people. I've asked my beloved what I can do to help. His response is, "pray, provide money to relief organizations, and plan to volunteer on the ground in the coming months when help will be the most useful."

An Invitation into Contemplative Expression…

In a quiet place, sit comfortably with your eyes closed. Take several deep breaths. Bring to mind a friend you know who is suffering. As you inhale, recognize and empathize with this person's pain. As you exhale, extend some sense of relief to this person, be it love, touch, care, resources. Repeat this process for several minutes, inhaling pain and exhaling relief. Next, as you inhale, recognize that there are many throughout the world suffering in this same situation as your friend. As you exhale, extend relief to all those who are suffering. Repeat this process for several minutes, inhaling the recognition of global difficulties and exhaling relief to the larger community.

Connected Breath
(Ar-Razzaq)

Breathing a Community of Peace

Islam

*Say: Who gives you sustenance
from the heaven and the earth?
Or Who controls the hearing
and the sight? And Who
brings forth the living from
the dead, and brings forth
the dead from the living?
And Who regulates the affairs?
Then they will say: Allah.*
Qur'an, 10.31

Christianity

*Now we have received not the
spirit of the world, but the
Spirit which is from God, that
we might understand the gifts
bestowed on us by God.*
1 Corinthians 2:12

Judaism

*By the word of the Lord the
heavens were made, and all their
host by the breath of his mouth.*
Psalms 33:6

O ne morning I awoke listening to Maya, my faithful canine companion, snoring in the corner of my bedroom. As I listened to her melodic rhythm, I felt a gratitude for the simple things in life—the sound of hearing a loved one's presence. I can forget these beautiful graces I am blessed with each day when I'm caught up in the busyness of life. It's really worthwhile to take a moment, or ten, or as many as it requires, to step back, center oneself, and breathe.

We all breathe the same air that circulates through our bodies, out of mine and into yours, out of yours and into mine. This breath creates a shared experience, a sense of community we may not notice, understand, or even accept…but it is still present.

In my experience, I feel each breath originating with the Divine's love. Inhaling that love into my body multiple times each minute reminds me that at any moment during the day I can slow down, focus on my breath, and feel the Divine's love radiating through my body. I breathe from my body to yours, and from yours to mine, forming an inspired community of peace.

Dear Loved Ones…

Where does your breath originate and begin its invitation to connect? Who and what are the blessed sounds in your life? When you focus on your breath, what do you discover? What brings you back to grace after being caught in the busyness of life?

An Invitation into Contemplative Expression…

Find a quiet place to lie down comfortably. Place your left hand on your belly and your right hand on your chest. Breathe normally feeling the rise and fall of your belly and your chest as you inhale and exhale. Inhale deeply and pull your breath into your belly until it is full, then inhale a bit further and expand your chest with breath as well. Hold your inhale for two counts. Exhale collapsing your belly, allowing the breath to leave first your belly and then your lungs. Hold your exhale for two counts. Repeat this pattern three or four times, feeling the rhythm of breath cycle as you inhale and exhale. Breathe normally, and experience the deep sensation of relaxation. Experience your breath extending beyond yourself and connecting to others.

Opening
(Al-Fattah)

Meet Me in the Middle

Meet me in the middle
Trusting what we've said
Feeling our way through this

Opening the doorway
Walking through with grace
Holding out for wonder

Traveling through nowhere
and everywhere in time
Seeking our resistance
and letting go of mine…
    and yours

All of the awakening
Is happening right now
All for us to ponder

Stepping into splendor
Face to face with love
Being in the moment

Many ways to do this
Some lead far apart
Others bring us closer

I'm offering my hand
With space enough for all
To meet me in the middle

Traveling through nowhere
and everywhere in time
Seeking our resistance
and letting go of mine…
    and yours

Meet me in the middle
Face to face with love

Opening

Dear Loved Ones...

Where do you find open doorways leading into love? How does it feel to walk through these doorways? What are the areas of resistance in your life that keep you from responding to the invitation of opening? Who are you hoping to meet in the middle?

An Invitation into Contemplative Expression...

Find a quite place to sit that feels balanced to you. Close your eyes and breathe deeply, inhaling and exhaling slowly. Place your hand on your heart and feel your chest expand and contract. Working with the phrase "opening to love," imagine that your heart is opening a bit wider with each breath, creating more space for love to enter. Notice what you feel emotionally and physically. Tone the sounds "oh-eh-ee-oh-oh-eh" and sense those vibrations in your chest through your hand. Afterward, journal about what it means to you to open further to a more expansive love.

The Opening

In the name of Allah, the Beneficent, the Merciful.

All praise is due to Allah, the Lord of the Worlds.
The Beneficent, the Merciful.
Master of the Day of Judgment.
Thee do we serve and Thee do we beseech for help.
Keep us on the right path.
The path of those upon whom Thou hast bestowed favors.
Not (the path) of those upon whom Thy wrath is brought down,
nor of those who go astray.

—Qur'an, 1.1–6

Honoring
(Al-Muizz)

Honoring Ourselves

I've been examining the concept of being present to what is, responding to reality, and the triggers that interfere with this. I'm wondering why it is that we often cannot see the blessings and gifts in front of us and instead focus on what we do not have. I believe it is because we think reality is supposed to be different than what we are experiencing. Our expectations of what should be can overwhelm and diminish our present situations. The abundance of life becomes overshadowed by a perceived scarcity.

I liken this feeling to peering into a full refrigerator when we are hungry, seeing a host of items, and deciding that we want something else. Our decision could be based on not knowing how to pull those ingredients together to make a meal. It could be that we were disappointed with what we found or that we imagine we need something other than what is in front of us. Maybe we crave something we assume will be tastier, or perhaps we need to satisfy an outside expectation. Our reaction, which may occur unconsciously in a fraction of a second, might include all of these elements.

So, rather than looking at what we have to work with and preparing a nourishing meal, we seek fulfillment from beyond what we have. We'll expend effort, perhaps a tremendous amount of it, attempting to satisfy our hunger. We'll go to the store, to a restaurant, or to a friend's home in search of what we believe will settle our cravings. We avoid the opportunity to work with what we have or what we have chosen. We avoid the challenge of responding to what is in front of us.

What if, instead, we peered into the refrigerator, saw the items there, and accepted the array of possibilities inviting us into creativity? What if we took a deep breath and responded to that invitation—to create a wonderful, tasty, nourishing meal?

Being present and responding to what is in front of us honors ourselves, our surroundings, and our gifts. It also honors the abundance of life, all that we have been given, and allows us to appreciate each other more fully. I invite you to notice and respond to the gifts life is offering you.

An Invitation into Contemplative Expression...

With art materials in hand, find a quiet, comfortable place to sit. Close your eyes and take several deep breaths, inhaling and exhaling slowly. Bring to mind the people and places you were present to during the past week. Notice which of these encounters you honored, and those where you felt honored, too. Open your eyes and draw each of these encounters inside your refrigerator. Select which of these events was most meaningful for you, and if you are able, contact that person and let them know the impact they had on your life.

Insights About Honoring from the Abrahamic Faiths

Islam
This is of the grace of my Lord that He may try me whether I am grateful or ungrateful; and whoever is grateful, he is grateful only for his own soul, and whoever is ungrateful, then surely my Lord is Self-sufficient, Honored.
Qur'an, 27.40

Christianity
Let love be genuine; hate what is evil, hold fast to what is good; love one another with brotherly affection; outdo one another in showing honor.
Romans 12:9–10

Judaism
For my brethren and companions' sake I will say, "Peace be within you!"
Psalms 122:8

Justice
(Al-Adl)

Redefining Vulnerability

Islam

*Say: My Lord has enjoined justice,
and set upright your faces at every
time of prayer and call on Him,
being sincere to Him in obedience;
as He brought you forth in the
beginning, so shall you also return.*
Qur'an, 7.29

Christianity

*For God shows no partiality. All
who have sinned without the law
will also perish without the law,
and all who have sinned under the
law will be judged by the law. For
it is not the hearers of the law who
are righteous before God, but the
doers of the law who
will be justified.*
Romans 2:11-13

Judaism

*Justice, and only justice, you shall
follow, that you may live and
inherit the land which the Lord
your God gives you.*
Deuteronomy 16:20

Justice chose me one morning on my way out the door for a walk in the rain. I was dressed in my "bee suit" as I refer to it, my bright yellow raingear, since there was a steady downpour. The walk was delightful, and the rain ran down the bridge of my nose though the rest of me was toasty and dry. I listened to the sound my boots made on the wet pavement and the greater cacophony of cars driving through puddles, tire treads parting the seas momentarily. As I walked, I pondered. What might I be processing, healing, or understanding by contemplating and painting justice today?

On the walk, I recalled several intense dreams I had experienced the previous night, one bordering on a nightmare. In this dream, a process server, a stranger claiming to represent someone intent on harming me, served me papers. The papers ordered me to appear in court over a matter that had nothing to do with me. My response was to deny that I was the person the process server was looking for, but I realized quickly that he saw through my attempt to escape. I was disheartened that my response was to deny myself, to disappear, rather than stand up to what was clearly a mistake. I was also angry, frustrated that once again I was being harassed for something that was outside myself, my control, my responsibility. The desire to simply be left alone prompted my thought of folding in on myself. If I disappeared, maybe the issue would be taken up by those who were actually engaged in it.

In the next scene I was drinking a beer with friends in an outdoor café. I was boldly explaining my desire to confront my fears, to welcome an opportunity to stand before a judge and make my case, to have an independent third party render judgment on whether I had erred. I felt confident that this judgment would be impartial, for the betterment of all, and regardless of the outcome, would help me grow into more of who I am. It would also render my foe helpless in his attempt to harm me now and in the future.

In real life I have been grappling with the relationship between discomfort (either physical or psychic) and vulnerability. Historically, in my life, the feeling of vulnerability was either precipitated by, or quickly followed by, punishment. I developed an association between feeling vulnerable and trying to figure out what I had done wrong. What had I done to deserve being mistreated by those so much more powerful than me? The need to know, predict, and adjust my behavior accordingly was my method of coping. I often wondered where God was in these situations that were so unfair.

In the last several years I have redefined vulnerability in connection with love, relationship, and safety in my close walk with God. I have also fallen deeply in love with an amazing man who epitomizes the love God has for me. This love that originates with God and manifests in my beloved produces both incredible expansiveness and exposure for me, a profound vulnerability because of the depth of the love we share. At times, this exposure triggers in me a past pattern of fear, concern that if I feel this vulnerable—even from a feeling as wonderful as love—there may be something wrong. I react with an effort to "know," to be certain. Short of certainty, I can fall into a place of distrust over everything that seems unpredictable. In this state, I begin to doubt myself, love, and, ultimately, God. When I doubt God, everything begins to unravel.

My response to the vulnerability that arises from doubt has been to try to hide myself internally. From the outside, I go about my day as normal, but from the inside, I am frightened, feel helpless, and fear punishment. I struggle to figure out what I can do to make things right, to feel secure again, to take care of my needs. I can spiral into a frantic state of shoring up what I "know" and bracing myself against what I may have missed. I seek short-term solutions, anything that will ease the unknown and make me feel that I am all right again.

This response no longer works for me. I am too aware of its faults, its limitations, to actually resolve anything. It often compounds the problems and conceals the underlying issues by presupposing projected outcomes that do not exist. Now, I'd rather acknowledge the issues and churn in the discomfort until I understand what God is revealing to me and what is asking to be healed. This has much more of a sense of justice.

In painting Justice, I noticed that it was first presenting itself through a design void of straight lines. All the curves of the circles were wavy. Then came small squares, building blocks tumbling through wholeness. The blocks did not right themselves into any pattern, but continued to fall and land in the openings left by the intersecting circles.

The initial colors are those found in deep, clean water—blues and greens and purples. This is the type of water that washes away any impurities, holy water directly from its source with no interference. It leaves you cleansed to your soul, baptized into a state of renewal through forgiveness. The message from judgment is permission to be oneself to the fullest, the call to step into who we are without fear of reprisal. Softer hues followed, providing a ladder between the lower and higher planes, while gold bridged and balanced two sides. Browns grounded the piece in wholeness.

Dear Loved Ones...

What produces a feeling of vulnerability in your life? What is your response? How do you shore up your need for emotional justice, for placing things in order so that you feel balanced once more? How do you re-engage with the Divine after a period of vulnerability and self-doubt?

An Invitation into Contemplative Expression...

With a loved one, find a quiet spot in nature. Sit down and notice your surroundings—sights, sounds, and sensations. Taking turns, describe to each other what you see, hear, and feel. Take your time. Be as descriptive as possible. Next, gaze deeply into each other's eyes. Again, describe what you see, hear, and feel. When you both are finished, notice whether you neglected to share that thing that makes you feel vulnerable and how this might relate to emotional justice. Dance the expression of this vulnerability, then say what needs to be spoken.

Awareness
(Al-Khabir)

Fostering the Present Moment

Dearly Beloved Divine,

How do I accept the notion of continuous change and its resulting impermanence while maintaining that You are aware of all? I struggle sometimes with the paradoxical notion of being on Your path, ever straying from that path, and yet always being exactly where I need to be in Your presence. There is a tremendous freedom in knowing that wherever I am, it is the perfect place to be, and that in the next moment I will be in the next perfect place because I am walking with You.

I often get caught in limited thinking, a sense that the difficult condition I am in will never change or a hope that a wonderful state will last forever. Both of these desires are incomplete. In the realm of impermanence, life continues to unfold moment by moment. Being present to each moment—living, breathing, experiencing, and accepting one moment at a time—allows us to experience Your ever-abiding awareness.

Faith encourages me to experience and follow the alignment of Your power within and beyond myself, to be led by what resonates deeply inside me, and to become wholly who I am. Within me resides a still point that connects me to something greater than my body, which is the essence of my being, the divine that exists within. Your attentiveness to my faith, my walk, and my essence is forever. You will always welcome me and help me mature into wakefulness.

Dear Loved Ones…

How do you respond to change while knowing that the Divine is aware of all? When do you experience limited thinking, hoping that something will change quickly or last forever? How do you foster being present in each moment? Where do you find your still point, your connection to the Divine?

An Invitation into Contemplative Expression…

With pen and paper in hand, find a quiet place to sit comfortably, preferably in nature. Close your eyes and observe your breathing, noticing the inhalations and exhalations. As you inhale, count "one." As you exhale, count "two." Continue breathing normally for several minutes counting "one" and then "two," "one" and then "two," with the rhythm of your breath. Next, slowly open your eyes. Take in everything around you through your awareness in the present moment. Notice what you see, hear, sense, and feel. When you are ready, write a poem or journal entry that captures this awareness.

Gratitude
(Ash-Shakur)

An Antidote to "Not Enough"

I'm teaching several classes at a local university, and one focuses on helping young people understand how the choices they make in their everyday lives affect the world. Besides discussing globalization and consumerism, we are delving into the subject of media influence. Media messages influence how we view our self-worth, how we spend our resources, how we assess others, and how we interact with the world.

As I've listened to my students, I've realized anew that many of us have lost touch with how deeply our personal choices are influenced by the media. We all know that the advertising industry does its best to manipulate our decisions through enticing commercials. Do we really need pizza at 11:30 p.m.? Is this what our body actually needs, or was our dinner earlier in the evening enough to energize us? Without the commercial's allure, would we have even considered ordering a pizza? In a similar vein, do we really need all the gadgets, toys, clothes, and other material goods advertised? Are we really going to look that good or have that much fun, simply because we buy a product?

I have not owned a television or watched TV for several years. This single decision has greatly reduced my desire to purchase items and has helped me to better understand true need. I also have much more time for everything else in my life that is important to me.

Media outlets can profoundly affect our everyday opinions and decisions. Even the most reputable and well-respected programs contain subtle and effective forms of advertising. Public radio announcers encourage the audience to visit the sponsor's website. When I hear that a story is sponsored by an organization, foundation, or commercial enterprise, I find myself wondering what authority the sponsor had in crafting that story, if any. My personal preference for news is the BBC, British Broadcasting Company, because of its global focus. Even so, I attempt to compare what I hear with other reputable news outlets to ensure a balanced perspective.

Who and what we listen to informs what we believe and can shape our choices. The media perpetuates our fear of scarcity, and at its core, our fear that we do not measure up. Rather than accepting who we are, we are taught that we need to be something else or someone different. It erodes our sense of self-worth, our internal values of integrity, kindness, compassion, love, and service, and leaves us feeling empty. The media then attempt to convince us that purchasing their sponsors' products will fill that void in our soul and move us toward becoming enough.

The antidote to "not enough" or scarcity thinking is gratitude. Giving thanks for what we have shifts us to an attitude of abundance, a place where we can embrace ourselves and each other as we are. In gratitude, we can cultivate the worth of our soul-based values and share these personal assets with others. In gratitude, we let go of our fears of scarcity and embrace a position of plenty, of enough. In gratitude, we recognize that what we truly need is typically provided for us without consternation or struggle. In gratitude, our personal choices change from consuming to sharing.

Dear Loved Ones...

Who are you listening to? Is this influence healthy? What leads you to scarcity thinking? What leads you to abundance thinking? When was the last time you expressed gratitude for all that you are?

An Invitation into Contemplative Expression...

Once a day for a month, document an event that made you feel fulfilled because it was "enough." This might be something you witnessed, such as a kind act, or something you experienced, such as finding relief in a good conversation with a friend, or something in which you participated, such as healing prayer for a loved one. Detail your gratitude and the ripple effects that may have extended beyond you. After each entry, take time to fully experience the feeling of gratitude and remind yourself that you are more than enough; you are a child of the Divine.

Praise the Lord!
Praise the Lord from the heavens,
praise him in the heights!
Praise him, all his angels,
praise him, all his host!

Praise him, sun and moon,
praise him, all you shining stars!
Praise him, you highest heavens,
and you waters above the heavens!
Let them praise the name of the Lord!

For he commanded and they were created.
And he established them for ever and ever;
he fixed their bounds which cannot be passed.

Praise the Lord from the earth,
you sea monsters and all deeps,
fire and hail, snow and frost,
stormy wind fulfilling his command!

Mountains and all hills,
fruit trees and all cedars!
Beasts and all cattle,
creeping things and flying birds!
Praise the Lord!

—Psalms 148:1–10

Highest Good
(Al-Ali)

The Breath of God

All Things Bright and Beautiful

All things bright and beautiful,
All creatures great and small,
All things wise and wonderful:
The Lord God made them all.

Each little flower that opens,
Each little bird that sings,
He made their glowing colors,
He made their tiny wings.

The rich man in his castle,
The poor man at his gate,
He made them, high or lowly,
And ordered their estate.

The purple headed mountains,
The river running by,
The sunset and the morning
That brightens up the sky.

The cold wind in the winter,
The pleasant summer sun,
The ripe fruits in the garden,
He made them every one.

The tall trees in the greenwood,
The meadows where we play,
The rushes by the water,
To gather every day.

He gave us eyes to see them,
And lips that we might tell
How great is God Almighty,
Who has made all things well.

—By Cecil Francis Alexander

Highest Good

Dear Loved Ones...

Where do you find brightness and beauty in your life? In the busyness of life, what might you do to see and take in all of creation around you? How might you express gratitude for your senses?

An Invitation into Contemplative Expression...

With your art materials close by, find a quiet space to sit and center yourself with your breathing. Notice how your chest and abdomen expand and contract with each breath. Close your eyes and take several deep breaths. Working with your five senses—sight, smell, taste, touch, and sound—notice your surroundings. For each sense, create a visual representation of what you are experiencing. When finished, consider whether the elements of the five drawings relate to each other.

Evening Prayer for the Sabbath

In this moment of silent communion with Thee,
O Lord, a still small silent voice speaks in the depth of my spirit.

It speaks to me of the things I must do
to attain holy kinship with Thee and to grow in the likeness of Thee.

I must do my allotted task with unflagging faithfulness
even though the eye of no taskmaster is on me.

I must be gentle in the face of ingratitude
or when slander distorts my noblest motives.

I must come to the end of each day
with a feeling that I have used its gifts gratefully and faced its trials bravely.

O Lord, help me to be ever more like Thee,
holy for Thou art holy, loving for Thou art love.

Speak to me, then, Lord, as I seek Thee again and again
in the stillness of meditation,
until Thy bidding shall at last become for me
a hallowed discipline, a familiar way of life.

—A Prayer from the Jewish Liturgy

Nourishment
(Al-Muqit)

Mystery from the Start

Insights About
Nourishment from the
Abrahamic Faiths

Islam

*So let them serve the Lord of this House.
Who feeds them against hunger and
gives them security against fear.*
Qur'an, 106.3–4

Christianity

*For the bread of God is that which
comes down from heaven, and gives life
to the world. They said to him, "Lord,
give us this bread always." Jesus said to
them, "I am the bread of life; he who
comes to me shall not hunger, and he
who believes in me shall never thirst."*
John 6:33–35

Judaism

*The Lord upholds all who are falling,
and raises up all who are bowed down.
The eyes of all look to thee, and thou
givest them their food in due season.
Thou openest thy hand, thou satisfiest
the desire of every living thing.*
Psalms 145:14–16

I've been praying for a long time
  that I might find
    someone like you.
Now that you are near me
  I see more clearly
    that it might come true.

How can this be
  a love so willingly
    given from the heart.
You're the answer to a prayer
  a gift precious and rare
    a mystery from the start.

And I don't know what to do
  with all this love that keeps pouring through.
And I don't know what to say
  to help us understand it's just this way.

Your voice calms all my shadows
  that lay in gallows
    from history.
Your smile lights up my senses
  my body dances
    with joy and glee.

We're moving to a symphony
  of love deliciously
    growing with time.
As we enter these new grounds
  we're invited to the sound
    of love divine.

Nourishment

Dear Loved Ones…

Where do you find the mystery of love? In what ways does this love nourish you? How will you share nourishment with others? Whom do you pray it will find? What pours through you?

An Invitation into Contemplative Expression…

With paper and pen in hand in a quiet space, find your breath. Breathe slowly, inhaling and exhaling. Close your eyes and relax your body. Consider the mystery within your life, particularly the mystery that comes with loving someone and being loved. This "someone" could be human, an animal companion, or the Divine. Focus your attention on one "someone" and notice the sensations that arise around your love for them. Allow words to form that might express this love. As the words come, write them down. After awhile, using the individual words and phrases you captured, create a poem expressing the mystery of your shared love.

Pir

Inspirer of my mind,
consoler of my heart,
healer of my spirit,
Thy presence lifteth me from earth to heaven,
Thy words flow as the sacred river,
Thy thought riseth as a divine spring,
Thy tender feelings waken sympathy in my heart.

Beloved Teacher,
Thy very being is forgiveness.
The clouds of doubt and fear are scattered
by Thy piercing glance.
All ignorance vanishes in Thy illuminating presence.
A new hope is born in my heart
by breathing Thy peaceful atmosphere.

O inspiring Guide through life's puzzling ways,
in Thee I feel abundance of blessing.

Amen.

—Prayer by Pir Hazrat Inayat Khan

Listening
(Al-Mujib)

The Breath of God

Canine Jailbreak

I'm practicing listening.

Closest to me I hear the nails on my dog's paws
scraping the wooden porch floor as she
optimistically searches for microscopic bits of non-existent food.

Slightly farther I hear her breath,
panting as she expresses her frustration
of not finding any crumb or other item that might be worth inhaling.

Slightly farther I hear the cicadas singing
their vibrational songs in the shadows of the sunshine,
beating their wings to attract a lover.

Slightly farther I hear the maple tree leaves
dancing in the breeze, dried seedpods clicking against each other
before twirling their way to the ground.

Slightly farther I hear the laughter of children
playing tag in their backyard yelling "You're it!"
then squealing as they try to flee.

Slightly farther I hear my neighbors
in conversation while tossing their recyclable cans
into the bin next to their front door.

Slightly farther I hear the sound of a car
winding its way along a curvy road, the brakes
grinding just a touch as they negotiate a sharp bend.

Slightly farther I hear the motor of a yard machine,
a leaf blower or weed trimmer or chainsaw,
it is too far to distinguish as they sound much the same.

Slightly farther I hear the compressed drone
of vehicles on a busy highway, a mile or two or five away.

Suddenly…two neighborhood dogs have escaped
their fenced-in yard—two labs,
one yellow and his brother chocolate brown.
Tearing down my street they celebrate a newly found freedom,
barking loudly, they encourage their neighborhood brethren to join their caper.

Now all I hear are dogs barking everywhere,
on all sides of me, drowning out all other sounds.
Maya on my porch, Kaas and her cousin next door,
Joe across the street, and countless others behind
the open window screens of their homes—so many that
their individual barks become difficult to distinguish.

The cacophony of canine voices overtakes everything.
What power! What beauty! What celebration!
What freedom of expression!

On a typical day, all of this—the rustling leaves,
the carefree children, the mating insects, the canine jailbreak,
the signs of life—might have registered as just background noise.

I'm so glad I'm practicing listening.

Dear Loved Ones…

When you take a moment to get quiet, what do you hear? Who makes the joyous sounds in your life? Where do the sounds of freedom arise for you? How might you practice listening?

An Invitation into Contemplative Expression…

With a trusted friend, sit facing one another in a relaxed manner. With eyes closed, hold hands and begin to feel each other's warmth and energy. After a few minutes, open your eyes and gaze deeply at each other. "Listen" to your souls speaking to one another. After a while, write down what you have "heard" and share it with your friend. Speak in "I" statements, as in "I heard…." Once the information is conveyed, let it go.

For the Lord gives wisdom;
from his mouth come knowledge and understanding;
he stores up sound wisdom for the upright;
he is a shield to those who walk in integrity,
guarding the paths of justice
and preserving the way of his saints.

Then you will understand righteousness and justice
and equity, every good path;
for wisdom will come into your heart,
and knowledge will be pleasant to your soul.

—Proverbs 2:6–10

Wisdom
(Al-Hakim)

Wisdom of the Desert

Insights About Wisdom from the Abrahamic Faiths

Islam

Whatever is in the heavens and the earth declares the glory of Allah, and He is the Mighty, the Wise.
Qur'an, 57.1

Christianity

For he has made known to us in all wisdom and insight the mystery of his will, according to his purpose which he set forth in Christ as a plan for the fullness of time, to unite all things in him, things in heaven and things on earth.
Ephesians 1:9–10

Judaism

O Lord, how manifold are thy works! In wisdom hast thou made them all; the earth is full of thy creatures.
Psalms 104:24

The Desert Fathers and Mothers sought solitude in community, relinquished worldly possessions, refrained from theological debate, and separated themselves from the noise of society—all so that they might enter a state through which to receive the Divine. We too become who we are as we stay present, receive God's signs, and give up our self—our need to know, predict, control, and consume. Only then can we recognize where the Divine is leading us in every moment.

These hermits recognized their obligation to pull the whole world to safety. They were not simply saving themselves through their rigorous dedication, but rather creating a foothold for all to follow. Similar to the Buddhist Bodhisattva's devotion to the enlightenment of all creatures, a monk's vow was not complete until the Kingdom of God reigned on earth.

One of my favorite stories is that of the disciple who gave money to anyone who insulted him during a three-year period. After three years had passed, the next person to insult him made him laugh. When asked why he was not offended, the monk responded "For three years I have been paying for this thing and now you provide it for nothing." What a blessing to recognize God's gifts and celebrate with laughter.

Dear Loved Ones...

Where do you seek solitude with the Divine? What deserts of wisdom are calling to you? Where is the Divine leading you? How do you celebrate God's gift of wisdom?

An Invitation into Contemplative Expression...

With a trusted friend, begin in a room large enough to move around comfortably. Put on soothing music that will support gentle movement. Stand facing each other. Touch the tip of your right index finger to your friend's right index finger so that you have one point of connection. Begin to lead your friend gently around the room simply through your fingertip. Then allow your friend to lead you around the room in the same way. After awhile, allow the leading and the following to flow between the two of you. Notice how it feels to lead, to be led, to flow back and forth. When you are finished, journal about how the experience contributes to your sense of wisdom.

Truth
(Al-Haqq)

Sacred Connections

A connection has been made.

It is beyond logic, beyond emotion,
beyond expectation, beyond judgment.

It is holy, a gift directly from God,
illustrating once again the exquisite oneness,
the merging that takes place within sacred connections.

It is pure and innocent, from the heart,
but beyond love with a small "l."

It is unconditional, without attachment, without outcome,
without predictability or control or calculation.

How does God manifest Herself
if not through these energetic, sacred connections?

How do we feel Spirit if not through the heart opening
to the full breadth of wonderment?

How can we possibly turn away from divinely inspired gifts,
or judge their worthiness or timelines or convenience?

When Spirit speaks, our world as we know it transforms.

Dear Loved Ones...

What sacred connections do you experience in your own life? How do you embrace these connections? Where do you share these holy invitations into truth?

An Invitation into Contemplative Expression...

With paper and pen in hand, take a long walk in nature. Find a quiet glen or stream or forest and rest. Take in all that you are witnessing and feel your truth in the presence of the Divine. Notice how Spirit speaks to you. Receive a poem that reflects the sacred connections in your life. Share the poem with someone you love.

Strength
(Al-Qawi)

How Shall We Live

I've noticed that the winds still blow
Even when I want it to be calm.
I cast about for stillness in the whirlwind
That surrounds me then I'm gone.
I seek to stay inside myself
Until I know the road that I should take.
But everyday I hear your call
To step into the risk for goodness' sake.

You move us out of comfort zone
Into some place that's unknown, to me.
You fling the doors open wide
And then ask us to step inside, with you.
You show us what we need to be
And ask us to participate fully.
You instigate, facilitate, coordinate
The change you want to see.

How shall we live to be the best of you,
To offer up ourselves in everything we do?
How shall we live to share the love we have,
To illuminate the path in everything we do?
How shall we live? Help us to hear you.

We argue with you til no end
Defending actions not taken in strife.
We walk away from need and pain,
Allowing greed to dominate our life.
We overlook the simple things
That hope would find inspiring, then pray,
"Tell me what it is you feel
I ought to be engaging in today."

Strength

Open up my eyes to see
Reality that stands before me now.
Move my heart from hesitation
Into a configuration, now.
Change my narrow point of view
In what it is I feel that I can do.
Humble me in gratitude
That I will follow servitude for you.

How shall we live to be the best of you,
To offer up ourselves in everything we do?
How shall we live to share the love we have,
To illuminate the path in everything we do?
How shall we live? Help us to hear you.

Dear Loved Ones...
What winds are blowing in your life indicating coming change? How will you respond to these winds? Where is your path illuminated? How will you share your strength, inner conviction, and all that you are, in love?

An Invitation into Contemplative Expression...
With a trusted friend, find a comfortable place to sit facing each other. Share one thought at a time with each other about how you wish to live your life—beginning with you, then alternating. Speak truthfully and listen deeply. When you are finished exchanging your wishes, select music and dance your desires for a life of change, illumination, and love.

Be Thou My Vision

Be Thou my Vision, O Lord of my heart;
Naught be all else to me, save that Thou art.
Thou my best Thought, by day or by night,
Waking or sleeping, Thy presence my light.

Be Thou my Wisdom, and Thou my true Word;
I ever with Thee and Thou with me, Lord;
Thou my great Father, I Thy true son;
Thou in me dwelling, and I with Thee one.

Be Thou my battle Shield, Sword for the fight;
Be Thou my Dignity, Thou my Delight;
Thou my soul's Shelter, Thou my high Tower:
Raise Thou me heavenward, O Power of my power.

Riches I heed not, nor man's empty praise,
Thou mine Inheritance, now and always:
Thou and Thou only, first in my heart,
High King of Heaven, my Treasure Thou art.

High King of Heaven, my victory won,
May I reach Heaven's joys, O bright Heaven's Sun!
Heart of my own heart, whatever befall,
Still be my Vision, O Ruler of all.

—Irish Folk Song

Deep Friendship
(Al-Wali)

Amazing Grace

Amazing grace! How sweet the sound
That saved a wretch like me!
I once was lost, but now am found;
Was blind, but now I see.

'Twas grace that taught my heart to fear,
And grace my fears relieved;
How precious did that grace appear
The hour I first believed!

Through many dangers, toils and snares,
I have already come;
'Tis grace hath brought me safe thus far,
And grace will lead me home.

The Lord has promised good to me,
His Word my hope secures;
He will my Shield and Portion be,
As long as life endures.

Yea, when this flesh and heart shall fail,
And mortal life shall cease,
I shall possess, within the veil,
A life of joy and peace.

The earth shall soon dissolve like snow,
The sun forbear to shine;
But God, who called me here below,
Will be forever mine.

When we've been there ten thousand years,
Bright shining as the sun,
We've no less days to sing God's praise
Than when we'd first begun.

—Song by John Newton

Insights About Deep Friendship from the Abrahamic Faiths

Islam
*Now surely the friends of Allah—
they shall have no fear nor
shall they grieve.*
Qur'an, 10.62

Christianity
*Peace be to you. The friends greet
you. Greet the friends,
every one of them.*
3 John 1:15

Judaism
*Thus the Lord used to speak to
Moses face to face, as a man
speaks to his friend.*
Exodus 33:11

Deep Friendship

Dear Loved Ones...

How do you balance loving someone deeply and granting them the space they need to expand? What allows you to give your heart openly without losing yourself in the process? How do you befriend and protect yourself, assert your own needs and take responsibility for meeting those needs?

An Invitation into Contemplative Expression...

Gather a group of friends for an evening of exploration and sharing. Ask your friends to bring a poem that describes what friendship means to them. With respect and honor, share your poems one at a time. After each poem discuss how the poem speaks to friendship and what that means to you. Celebrate your friendship with gratitude in knowing each other.

O Lord, thou hast searched me and known me!
Thou knowest when I sit down and when I rise up;
thou discernest my thoughts from afar.
Thou searchest out my path and my lying down,
and art acquainted with all my ways.

Even before a word is on my tongue,
lo, O Lord, thou knowest it altogether.
Thou dost beset me behind and before,
and layest thy hand upon me.

Such knowledge is too wonderful for me;
it is high, I cannot attain it.
Whither shall I go from thy Spirit?
Or whither shall I flee from thy presence?

If I ascend to heaven, thou art there!
If I make my bed in Sheol, thou art there!
If I take the wings of the morning
and dwell in the uttermost parts of the sea,
even there thy hand shall lead me,
and thy right hand shall hold me.

—Psalms 139:1–10

Creation
(Al-Mubdi)

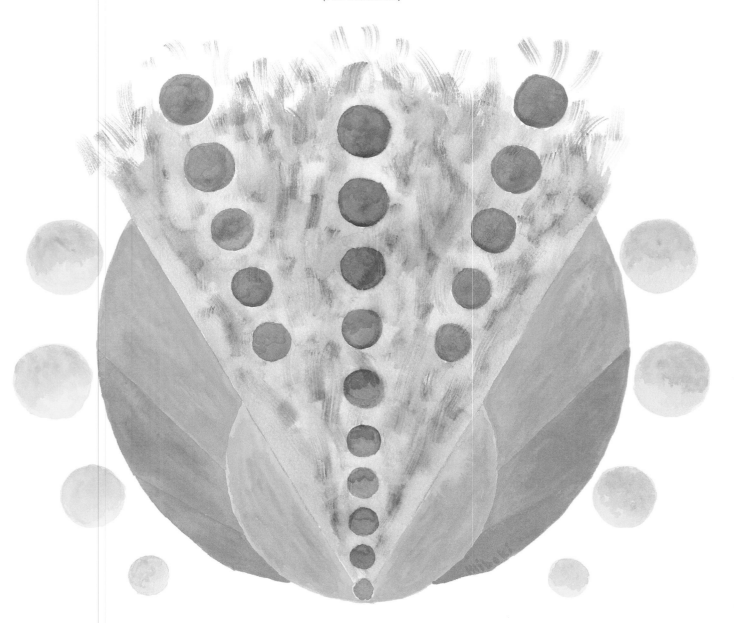

Love with All Your Might

Islam

*What! Do they not consider how Allah origi-
nates the creation, then reproduces it? Surely
that is easy to Allah. Say: Travel in the earth
and see how He makes the first creation,
then Allah creates the latter creation; surely
Allah has power over all things.*
Qur'an, 29.19–20

Christianity

*He is the image of the invisible God, the
first-born of all creation; for in him all
things were created, in heaven and on earth,
visible and invisible, whether thrones or
dominions or principalities or authorities—
all things were created through him and for
him. He is before all things, and in
him all things hold together.*
Colossians 1:15-17

Judaism

*For thus says the Lord, who created the
heavens (he is God!), who formed the earth
and made it (he established it; he did not
create it a chaos, he formed it to be inhab-
ited!): 'I am the Lord, and there is no other.'*
Isaiah 45:18

Feel my rhythm in your heartbeat
Feel my presence in your veins
Feel my love with you at all times
Know that I am just the same.

Sense that I am with you
Sense the longing in my heart
Sense the openness surrounding
Know that I will do my part.

Enter into my love for you
And radiate my light.
Be my presence within you
And love with all your might.

Touch the arms that reach out
Touch the goodness in your soul
Touch the one who stands before you
Know that I will make you whole.

Be the gift I wish to share
Be the warmth that shines each day
Be the invitation always
Know that I will guide the way.

An Invitation into Contemplative Expression...

With pen and paper in hand, find a quiet place to sit on a sunny day. Close your eyes and feel the sun's light. Take several deep breaths while welcoming this light to penetrate your body, warming you throughout. Imagine a loved one, perhaps someone in need of your love. While holding this being in your heart, allow the light and warmth that energizes your body to extend beyond you and reach your loved one. Imagine this light surrounding them, warming them, filling them with radiant love. Next, write a letter to this loved one letting them know how much you love and care for them.

Death
(Al-Mumit)

Gatekeeper

The heart is a gatekeeper of death.

To accept loss, the heart recognizes
 what no longer works,
 what has come to pass,
 what is asking to die in us.

It is a sacred dance, entering the heart,
 a time of transition,
 a sense of impermanence,
 an indication of change.

This ephemeral dance illuminates
 that which we resist and
 that which we embrace,
 that which causes pain and
 that which brings us joy,
 that which we discard and
 that for which we yearn.

It enters us into the flow
 of comprehending choices,
 of birthing desires,
 of craving permanence.

Embraced by the heart, death is an invitation
 to celebrate each moment,
 to respond to the fullness of life,
 to appreciate omnipresent gifts.

Death is a gatekeeper of the heart.

Insights About Death from the Abrahamic Faiths

Islam
His is the kingdom of the heavens and the earth; He gives life and causes death; and He has power over all things.
Qur'an, 57.2

Christianity
For if we have been united with him in a death like his, we shall certainly be united with him in a resurrection like his.
Romans 6:5

Judaism
For the waves of death encompassed me, the torrents of perdition assailed me; the cords of Sheol entangled me, the snares of death confronted me.
2 Samuel 22:5

An Invitation into Contemplative Expression…

With a friend, find a place to walk among the richness of the earth. As you stroll, share your current state of mind, all of what is feeding you and that which is causing you to struggle. With each other, share where you see the death and birth process in the other person. Discuss how allowing the old to find a resting place allows the new to come into being. Notice how loss, no matter how painful, can lead to transformative awakening. On completion, find a way to celebrate being together.

Intuition
(Al-Wajid)

A Time for Everything

For everything there is a season,
and a time for every matter under heaven:

A time to be born, and a time to die;
a time to plant, and a time to pluck up what is planted;
a time to kill, and a time to heal;
a time to break down, and a time to build up;

A time to weep, and a time to laugh;
a time to mourn, and a time to dance;
a time to cast away stones,
and a time to gather stones together;

A time to embrace, and a time to refrain from embracing;
a time to seek, and a time to lose;
a time to keep, and a time to cast away;
a time to rend, and a time to sew;

A time to keep silence, and a time to speak;
a time to love, and a time to hate;
a time for war, and a time for peace.

—Ecclesiastes 3:1–8

Dear Loved Ones...

What is time revealing to you in this season of your life? How does the impermanence of all influence what you experience? Knowing that this too shall pass, do your feelings reveal a sense of attachment, aversion, or detachment? How may you honor this moment, just as it is?

An Invitation into Contemplative Expression...

Ask a good friend to go on a walk with you outdoors in a natural setting. Bring a copy of this poem with you. As you walk, talk with each other about how the seasons in your life are expanding, contracting, or flowing. Take turns asking each other when you last experienced birth, death, being planted, being plucked, feeling killed, feeling healed.... Follow the flow of the poem. When you are finished, sit with each other and listen to the sounds of nature.

Insights About Intuition from the Abrahamic Faiths

Islam
He it is who sends down clear communications upon His servant, that he may bring you forth from utter darkness into light; and most surely Allah is Kind, Merciful to you.
Qur'an, 57.9

Christianity
In that same hour he rejoiced in the Holy Spirit and said, "I thank thee, Father, Lord of heaven and earth, that thou hast hidden these things from the wise and understanding and revealed them to babes; yea, Father, for such was thy gracious will."
Luke 10:21

Judaism
For the Lord gives wisdom; from his mouth come knowledge and understanding.
Proverbs 2:6

Unity
(Al-Wahid)

Stirred into Unity

Lately I have been feeling stirred,
struggling against expectations I have set for myself.
I'm not sure what those expectations are,
I just know that I am falling short of meeting them.
Crazy, huh!

Many of us are raised this way,
sensing that we are falling short
of who knows what, and never
quite understanding the rules.
That's because the rules were mostly random,
always changing, based on someone else's
needs, comfort level, mood.

The expectation was "control yourself."
The hidden message was that if we own and exert
our natural power, our physical energy,
our enormous creativity, our deep emotions,
something awful might happen.
The world might spin out of control and disintegrate.

The expectation was "pay attention, remain vigilant,
redouble your efforts, mold to the ideal."
The hidden message was that if we don't meet their rules,
their expectations, something awful might happen.
They might spin out of control and destroy us.

Our souls were both suffocated and abandoned.

Now I find myself walking with You, God,
filled with power, energy, creativity, emotion—
feeling to the very depths of my being
while soaring to the heights of grace.

There is no overt control, just a willingness
to surrender to Your leading even when,
perhaps especially when, I am unclear
where We are headed.

But there always is a "We."
Even when I forget that, as I have lately,
or separate temporarily from You,
the We remains.

Sometimes, when old expectations and rules invade,
when old patterns and confusion transpire,
I am afraid of compromising the We
by not hearing You, by not discerning properly,
by letting You down.
Yet simply Being is all You ask of me.
There are no timelines, no criteria, no hoops to jump through.
Rather, You invite the recognition of the We,
the surrender into Your love, the acceptance of Union.

My soul is stirred into aliveness and Unity.

Dear Loved Ones...

What expectations threaten your sense of unity? What rules do you continue to hold as true even though they are not yours? Where do you find the "We" that is always? How is your soul stirred into Unity?

An Invitation into Contemplative Expression...

Find a place to comfortably lie down in nature. Notice whether the place you choose is quiet and whether the space is open, such as a meadow or glen, or more contained, such as the woods or a nook by a stream. As you feel yourself in contact with the earth, allow your body to relax and feel the strength of the ground supporting you. Take several deep breaths, relaxing your body further, sinking into the space you have chosen. Listen to the sounds around you as you deepen into a peaceful state. When you are ready, begin to sing in concert with the sounds that you hear. Reflect on the harmonious sounds throughout the world.

Breathe on Me, Breath of God

Breathe on me, Breath of God,
fill me with life anew,
that I may love what thou dost love,
and do what thou wouldst do.

Breathe on me, Breath of God,
until my heart is pure,
until with thee I will one will,
to do and to endure.

Breathe on me, Breath of God,
till I am wholly thine,
till all this earthly part of me
glows with thy fire divine.

Breathe on me, Breath of God,
so shall I never die,
but live with thee the perfect life
of thine eternity.

—Song by Edwin Hatch

Inclusion
(Al-Ahad)

An Invitation to Heal

This morning my beloved read me one of his favorite poems by Charles Bukowski, "a wild, fresh wind blowing…." In it, Bukowski speaks about a childhood filled with his father's "raw and stupid hatred" of which he was often the recipient. At that time in his life, he thought his father's rage might have been unique. Then he stepped out into the world and found his father's angry "counterparts everywhere." He even lived with some of these counterparts, finding himself again on the receiving end of wounds and abuse.

It is not difficult to imagine, when raised in a household filled with rage or having survived a relationship riddled with abuse, how one might come to experience the world as a place of pain and punishment. Sometimes our religious institutions reinforce this idea by teaching that God is vengeful and punishes. Certainly texts quoted from the Old Testament, especially when taken out of context, can appear to support this claim. Other times our communities support the idea that the world is unsafe, that we must fear each other, and that people of different ethnicities, spiritual practices, socio-economic status—people who are not like us—deserve a wary eye. Our political and corporate leaders and institutions can bolster this discrimination by the laws they pass and the policies they create.

When we see the world through this lens, one of pain, fear, punishment, and exclusion, we can find evidence everywhere to support this claim. And though pain, fear, punishment, and exclusion exist, they need not dominate our sense of the essence of human beings, the environment, or the Divine. When we choose instead to view the world through a lens of love, grace, and gratitude, we begin to understand that every moment in life is a gift. Each moment is an invitation to heal, to transform our pain and woundedness, and to enter into our true nature of happiness and contentment. Through this inclusive orientation to the world, we perceive acts of kindness, love, selflessness, mercy, compassion, cooperation, forgiveness…all in ways that can contribute to healing ourselves, our institutions, our communities, and our planet.

One of the ways I remind myself that the world is filled with the Divine's essence is through contemplation. By sitting still, focusing on my breath, and calming my mind, I experience God's love, witness a world full of grace, sense my oneness with all, and express my gratitude for all the healing invitations that I can engage in each day. I shift from a place of agitation to one of lightness, from irritation to happiness, from control to contentment, from expectation to acceptance.

Insights About Inclusion from the Abrahamic Faiths

Islam

Say: *He, Allah, is One. Allah is He on Whom all depend. He begets not, nor is He begotten. And none is like Him.*
Qur'an, 112.1–4

Christianity

Finally, all of you, have unity of spirit, sympathy, love of the brethren, a tender heart and a humble mind.
1 Peter 3:8

Judaism

If there is among you a poor man, one of your brethren, in any of your towns within your land which the Lord your God gives you, you shall not harden your heart or shut your hand against your poor brother.
Deuteronomy 15:7

Inclusion

Bukowski concludes his poem by recognizing that, when allowed to appreciate the richness of life, he is a happy and content guy, so happy that the simple act of receiving a cup of coffee from a waitress feels like "a wild, fresh wind blowing…." What simple gesture would make you feel "a wild, fresh wind blowing"?

Dear Loved Ones…

Where do you find angry counterparts in your life? How do you contribute to those experiences? What is your method for transforming them? Who are the healing presences in your life? What healing invitations have you received or extended lately to create inclusion? When and how did you last express gratitude for the Divine's essence in the world?

An Invitation into Contemplative Expression…

Select a musical instrument of any kind. This might be as simple as using your voice as your musical instrument. Experiment with creating various tones, moving back and forth between harmonious and dissonant qualities. Sense the characteristics that these tones inspire in your body. Notice how your body shifts both physically and emotionally from one quality to the next.

My God and My Lord

Eyes are at rest, the stars are setting.
Hushed are the stirrings of birds in their nests,
Of monsters in the ocean.

You are the Just who knows no change,
The Balance that can never swerve,
The Eternal which never passes away.

The doors of Kings are bolted now and guarded by soldiers.
Your Door is open to all who call upon You.

My Lord,
Each love is now alone with his beloved.
And I am alone with You.

—Poem by Rabia al Basri

Refuge
(As-Samad)

For Tonight

Islam

And whoever flies in Allah's way, he will find in the earth many a place of refuge and abundant resources....
Qur'an, 4.100

Christianity

Come to me, all who labor and are heavy laden, and I will give you rest. Take my yoke upon you, and learn from me; for I am gentle and lowly in heart, and you will find rest for your souls. For my yoke is easy, and my burden is light.
Matthew 11:28–30

Judaism

The Lord is my rock, and my fortress, and my deliverer, my God, my rock, in whom I take refuge, my shield and the horn of my salvation, my stronghold and my refuge, my savior; thou savest me from violence. I call upon the Lord, who is worthy to be praised, and I am saved from my enemies.
2 Samuel 22:2–4

Stepping off the platform
Feeling so worn
As the evening flies.
Walking to my car door
Wondering what for
Staring at the sky.

Where you are seems to be
So much farther than I can see.
If I showed you with words unspoken
What it means to be unbroken.

Driving home at midnight
Among the starlight
Guiding my way.
Winding through the shadows
Looking for crossroads
Of what my heart might say...

Be with me my love
And from above
It will be all right.
Set your spirit free
And let it be
At least for tonight.

An Invitation into Contemplative Expression...

With art materials in hand, find a quiet place to sit comfortably. Close your eyes and breathe slowly. As you inhale, allow one word to emerge that describes what gives you a sense of refuge at this moment. As you exhale, allow one word to emerge that depicts the refuge, the protection you would like to offer the world. Continue to breathe normally, inhaling and exhaling these two one-word mantras—what you need and what you would like to offer the world. Allow a safe haven of love to form in and around you. Open your eyes and express in words or images this sanctuary.

Restoring Equilibrium
(At-Tawwib)

Relinquishing Self-Judgment, Restoring Equilibrium

I am reading Joan Halifax's book *Being with Dying*. I started it as my beloved left to attend the author's week-long educational retreat on the same topic at Upaya Zen Center in Santa Fe. I am also recovering from surgery, and as I read, I am deeply stirred by her message on being present and the healing that results from accepting what is.

In my current recovery, I am learning to respond to my body's needs rather than what I think is supposed to be happening. It's funny...typically, I am adamant about listening to my body's requests, but when I feel ill, I set that gift aside and revert to self-judgment, to body management. There is something about being ill, or in physical pain, that has never felt OK to me. I've always tried to resolve illness quickly, ignoring what my body requires for mending. Being ill, being in pain, being vulnerable doesn't feel safe. As soon as I can bear it, I override the pain or discomfort and move on. I cringe as I write this, feeling the cellular memories arise.

Again I struggle with judgment, with resistance, with letting go into what is. I realize that I have slipped into past patterns, judging myself based on my progress. I have constructed a story of how I am supposed to heal rather than attending to how I am indeed recovering. Yesterday I was in pain. I was bleeding heavily; I was nauseated, lightheaded, and dizzy. That was my experience and yet I felt it shouldn't be that way... not because pain or bleeding might indicate a problem, but because I simply felt I ought to be finished mending.

Judgment is counter to being present, being with what is. Telling ourselves stories about how things should be, and then struggling to control those circumstances, usurps the beauty, wonder, and mystery of what is. If reality is the gift...why do we resist it? Perhaps so we can avoid the judgment or shame involved with not meeting our own or someone else's expectations. Where is the shame in being present with and acknowledging reality? If reality varies from someone else's expectations, does that make it wrong? Reality is reality. It is what it is.

Resistance, stories, judgment, shame, and self-blame can all mask what is truly occurring. They all interfere with being present to the awareness of reality. One becomes focused on avoidance, using control and expectations to avoid pain or conflict. From this place of evasion, fear sits at the core of our decisions. Love is nowhere to be found, lost in the shadows of uncertainty.

Restoring Equilibrium

Judgment distorts reality. It moves us to a place of shame, and it weakens our ability to perceive clearly. Judgment creates a false sense of certainty, as though imposing "should" will control or guarantee the outcome. But uncertainty pervades everything. Letting go of judgment, embracing uncertainty, seeing clearly, experiencing the present, living into impermanence with kindness, compassion, joy, and equanimity…this is what Joan Halifax espouses. This is what prepares us both for living and dying fully.

This recovery process has been an unexpected blessing for me on many levels. It is teaching me how to be safe in a powerful way—internally, right to my core—by relinquishing judgment, embracing reality, and restoring equilibrium. I want to be present to the entire process, to notice how my body is mending, and to do so without judgment. I bask in the love of my supportive friends and attend to the ability the body has to restore itself. For this, I emit gratitude and accept the gift of being present.

Dear Loved Ones…

What judgments are you holding about yourself that interfere with your equilibrium? How might you let go of what "should be" happening in your life and embrace what is truly there? How do you participate in the gift of being present?

An Invitation into Contemplative Expression…

Find a comfortable place to lie down, such as the floor, a couch, or bed. Take several deep breaths, inhaling and exhaling, moving air into and out of your lungs. With your eyes closed, begin to tone "ah" and allow the sound to release any tension your body holds. After a few minutes, begin to tone "eh" and allow your mind to release any stress or worry. Next, tone "ee" and allow the sound to penetrate and awaken your soul. Finally, tone "oh" and allow the vibration to carry itself through your body, mind, and soul. Relax into the vibration and feel yourself restoring to equilibrium.

A Call to Prayer

Softly the evening vespers
Hallow the closing day;
Sweetly the Savior whispers,
"Come to the throne and pray."

Come, ere the shadows lengthen,
Bring Him thy burdened heart;
Come where His grace may strengthen,
Come from thy cares apart.

Smiles of His love await thee,
Lighting His lovely face;
Just to behold His beauty,
Dwell in the secret place.

Boldly we may approach Him,
Mercy and grace to own;
Tempted like us, He bid us
Come to the Father's throne.

Softly I hear Him calling,
Calling at close of day;
Sweetly His tones are falling,
"Come to the throne and pray."

—Poem by Clara M. Brooks

Enrichment
(Al-Mughni)

Shepherding Love

The Lord is my shepherd, I shall not want;
he makes me lie down in green pastures.

He leads me beside still waters;
he restores my soul.
He leads me in paths of righteousness
for his name's sake.

Even though I walk through
the valley of the shadow of death,
I will fear no evil;
for thou art with me;
thy rod and thy staff, they comfort me.

Thou preparest a table before me
in the presence of my enemies;
thou anointest my head with oil,
my cup overflows.

Surely goodness and mercy shall follow me
all the days of my life;
and I shall dwell in the house of the Lord forever.

—Psalm 23

Insights About Enrichment from the Abrahamic Faiths

Islam
…He it is Who enriches and gives to hold.
Qur'an, 53.48

Christianity
The point is this: he who sows sparingly will also reap sparingly, and he who sows bountifully will also reap bountifully. Each one must do as he has made up his mind, not reluctantly or under compulsion, for God loves a cheerful giver.
2 Corinthians 9:6–7

Judaism
For as the earth brings forth its shoots, and as a garden causes what is sown in it to spring up, so the Lord God will cause righteousness and praise to spring forth before all the nations.
Isaiah 61:11

Dear Loved Ones...

Who do you consider your shepherd and how do you offer yourself as a shepherd to others? What areas in your life require nourishment and enrichment?

An Invitation into Contemplative Expression...

With paper and pen in hand, find a quiet place to lie down. Close your eyes, take several deep breaths, and allow your body to relax. Feel the firmness of the ground supporting you. Imagine a time in your life when you were a shepherd to others, a time when you were able to support someone else as firmly as the ground is supporting you. Next, imagine another time when a friend or loved one provided shepherding for you, when you felt firmly held either physically or emotionally. When you are ready, open your eyes and write a poem reflecting both situations, depicting the blessings of providing and receiving shepherding.

Pain and Loss
(Ad-Darr)

Come to Me

Come to me…and rest your weariness
Come to me…and let your mind confess
Come to me…and step out of this mess
Come to me…and know that you are blessed

Come to me…and step in from the cold
Come to me…and break out of your mold
Come to me…and feel the peace I hold
Come to me…and let me fill your soul

I know that you are tired, I see it in your eyes
I know that you are broken, I hear it in your why's
I know that you are hurting, I feel it in your cries
I know that you are desperate, just too many good-byes

Come to me…and ease out of this place
Come to me…and open up a space
Come to me…and let the pain erase
Come to me…and be filled with my grace

Dear Loved Ones…

What pain or loss needs releasing so that you might let love in? Where are you carry-
ing exhaustion, brokenness, hurt, or desperation in your body? How do you respond
to the Divine's call for you to rest with grace?

An Invitation into Contemplative Expression…

Listen to soothing music. Lie down on the floor in an area with enough space to
move your body. Slowly, mentally scan your body and notice the location of any
tension or discomfort. Select one area of your body that needs to have pain or loss
released such as tension in your shoulders, discomfort in your belly, or pain in your
feet. Gently move or massage that body part while encouraging the area to relax,
release, and renew. Notice any thoughts, words, colors, or images that arise as you
are working on this area. Next, shift your focus to the next body part that needs
attention. Continue this practice with each of the uncomfortable areas in your body.
If you like, write down what you noticed.

Light
(An-Nur)

The Light Within

Islam

Do you not see that Allah makes the night to enter into the day, and He makes the day to enter into the night, and He has made the sun and the moon subservient to you; each pursues its course till an appointed time; and that Allah is Aware of what you do?
Qur'an, 31.29

Christianity

You are the light of the world. A city set on a hill cannot be hid. Nor do men light a lamp and put it under a bushel, but on a stand, and it gives light to all in the house. Let your light so shine before men, that they may see your good works and give glory to your Father who is in heaven.
Matthew 5:14–16

Judaism

And God said, "Let there be light;" and there was light. And God saw that the light was good; and God separated the light from the darkness. God called the light Day, and the darkness he called Night. And there was evening and there was morning, one day.
Gen 1:3–5

I'm the lightening strike,
I'm the fire that burns,
I'm the spark that ignites,
   The desire that churns.

I'm the invitation,
I'm the sacred ground,
I'm the light within,
   That's so profound.

Can you feel my body reaching out to you,
Searching for the knowledge to remember what is true?
Can you hear my whispers across this great divide,
Shouting out in silence to reach the other side?

Can you see my presence calling our your name,
Emitting all the love I can, relinquishing all pain?
Can you taste the afterwards of life that's come your way,
Breathing in the wonderment of each and every day?

Can you touch the stars and sense their light is clear?
Can you see the moon and know that I am near?
Can you feel the rhythm of love that pulses through?
Can you taste the innocence that life requires of you?

We're the lightening strike,
We're the fire that burns,
We're the spark that ignites,
   The desire that churns.

We're the invitation,
We're the sacred ground,
We're the light within,
   That's so profound.

Light

Dear Loved Ones...

How do you engage the light within? How do you feel, hear, see, taste, touch, and sense the Divine's gifts to you? What is required to breathe in the wonderment of each day? Where does the spark of desire reside in you?

An Invitation into Contemplative Expression...

With your art materials close by, find a quiet space to sit and center yourself with your breathing. Notice how your chest and abdomen expand and contract with each breath. Close your eyes and take several deep breaths. Imagine a column of light in your body between your belly and your throat. Notice the brightness of the light. Allow that light to grow brighter and to spread slowly throughout the rest of your body, migrating through your torso, into your arms and legs, down to the tips of your fingers and toes. Notice the sensation of the light energizing every part of your being. After awhile, open your eyes and create an artistic rendition of yourself infused with light.

The Verse of Light

Allah is the light of the heavens and the earth.
His light is as a niche in the wall
in which there is a lamp, the lamp is in a glass,
and the glass is as it were a brightly shining star,
lit from a blessed olive–tree,
neither eastern nor western,
the oil whereof almost gives light though fire touch it not.

Light upon light!
Allah guides to His light whom He pleases,
and Allah sets forth parables for men,
and Allah is Cognizant of all things.

—Qur'an, 24:35

Guidance
(Al-Hadi)

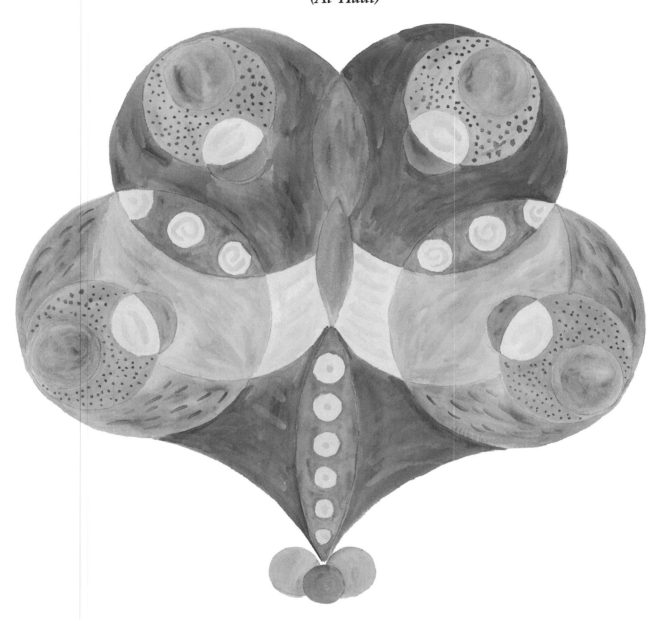

God Helps All

My experience with each of the Ninety-Nine Names of God has been unique, though in almost every instance that a Name chooses me, my urge to paint is immediate and I do my best to advance to the paper as soon as feasible, usually within the day. Al-Hadi, The Guide, or the characteristic "Guidance," was different. Even though I felt called to paint Guidance immediately, it actually took me more than two months to get to painting this name. During this time I moved through my daily living, sitting with Al-Hadi and allowing questions and insights about Guidance to surface.

The phrase "God helps those who help themselves" soon came to me. My parents taught me at a very young age that the idea of God helping those who helped themselves was from the Bible. I thought that God would only respond to me if I was completely self-sufficient and essentially needed nothing. I learned to take care of myself, anyone else's needs, and any situation that was not as expected. Because of this, I learned how to fix nearly any situation, solve any problem, and soon, how to predict and shape the future to avoid anything that might appear wrong—or so I thought.

I also had to be self-sufficient in love, loss, fear, sadness, joy…any emotion, whether positive or negative. As a small child, I felt it was up to me, that God would be absent if I could not take care of all of my needs, desires, and fears. And, if I slipped and found myself in need, God would immediately abandon me as unworthy of attention or assistance.

As an adult, I can see the inherent contradiction in the idea of God only responding when I don't need help. I'm guessing my well-intentioned parents were using "God helps those who help themselves" as a motivational tool to persuade me to complete my chores or to respond to their needs. However, interpreting this phrase as an indication of God's capriciousness has haunted me my entire life. Until the last few years, it shaped my view of God as fickle, unresponsive, manipulative, disinterested, and spiteful. If I was not completely accepting responsibility and committing my all, I presumed I was forsaken to struggle until I could pull myself back together. If I was ill, or hurt beyond what I could manage, God discarded me until I was well again.

God's ability (in my outlook) to connect or disconnect with me at will depending on my efforts, is of course, directly opposed to the notion of grace. I was also later reminded that "God helps those who help themselves" is not scripturally based, but

Guidance

comes to us by way of Benjamin Franklin (1736). Franklin was a deist and thus believed that God did not play an active role in our lives. From his point of view if man was not able to help himself, then man was hopeless. The Bible, the core of my religious instruction from a young age, clearly offered numerous illustrations of God helping those in need, particularly the poor and helpless. Often a determination of how godly a city or town was directly depended on the degree they cared for those in need. Jesus responds time and again to those asking for help and warns those who think they can go it alone.

Many books have been written about God's grace. The common theme is that God's love, guidance, and help are specifically not based on our own efforts. These gifts from God are unconditional, period. God is persistent, patient, and incessantly invitational. His unremitting love is offered to us in an endless stream of grace. We are the ones who separate ourselves from God, sometimes by misunderstanding who God is based on what we have been taught. God guides us to all that is good for the benefit and satisfaction of our needs. This uninterrupted guidance flows from God to us.

Our response requires faith, especially when we are confused, suffering, or feel led astray. Rather than stepping outside of yourself and expending tremendous effort to predict or control your future, I invite you to go inward, be silent, and listen to how God is guiding you. The guidance is at hand. Can you hear it? For me, it is a necessity to participate in this practice every day. My faith strengthens my ability to hear God's guidance, and following God's guidance strengthens my faith.

Dear Loved Ones...

What compels you to separate from the Divine into self-sufficiency? In what circumstances do you find yourself trying to handle things on your own? How do you find God's grace in your struggles? What strengthens your faith and brings you back to the Divine?

An Invitation into Contemplative Expression...

With paper and pen in hand, venture outdoors and find a quiet place in nature to sit. Begin by facing east. Notice any flora and fauna around you. Close your eyes, listen, and feel the air on your skin. Notice the sounds and sensations your body hears and feels. Ask yourself "What guidance do I need at this moment?" Meditate on this question and document any insights you receive. Repeat this process facing south, west, and north, and notice how the insights vary.

Khatum

Thou, Who art the Perfection
of Love, Harmony, and Beauty,
The Lord of heaven and earth,
open our hearts, that we may hear Thy Voice,
which constantly cometh from within.

Disclose to us Thy Divine Light,
which is hidden in our souls,
that we may know and understand life better.

Most Merciful and Compassionate God,
give us Thy great Goodness,
Teach us Thy loving Forgiveness,
Raise us above the distinctions and differences
which divide us,
Send us the Peace of Thy Divine Spirit,
And unite us all in Thy Perfect Being.

Amen.

—Prayer by Pir Hazrat Inayat Khan

Patience
(As-Sabur)

Unfolding to the Mystery

Insights About Patience
from the Abrahamic Faiths

Islam

*O you who believe! Seek
assistance through patience
and prayer; surely Allah is
with the patient.*
Qur'an, 2.153

Christianity

*The saying is sure and worthy
of full acceptance that Christ
Jesus came into the world to save
sinners. And I am the foremost
of sinners; but I received mercy
for this reason, that in me, as
the foremost, Jesus Christ might
display his perfect patience for
an example to those who were to
believe in him for eternal life.*
1 Timothy 1:15–16

Judaism

*The Lord is good to those who
wait for him, to the soul that
seeks him. It is good that one
should wait quietly for the
salvation of the Lord.*
Lamentations 3:25–26

Unfolding to the mystery
Letting go of what ought to be
And trusting that I will see
What's unfolding in the mystery

You came to me at the right time
You took my hand and said you're fine
You made it clear that your love would shine
And all you asked was that I make you mine

So lead me to serve your way
Guide me through my darkest day
Show me that it will be OK
And lift me with the words you say

Speak to me in a way that I can hear
Hold me in a way I feel you near
Love me in a way that's really clear
And wash me in a way that drowns my fears

Dear Loved Ones…

Where do you sense the presence of patience in your life? What is involved in your unfolding process? What support do you need during these times? Where do you find the patience and trust required to take the Divine's hand during your darkest days? What words lift you?

An Invitation into Contemplative Expression…

With art materials in hand, find a quiet place to sit comfortably. Close your eyes. Take several breaths, inhaling and exhaling slowly. Allow your mind to quiet itself and begin toning out loud the vowels for patience "ah–ee–eh–eh" slowly. Continue to repeat this toning phrase several times until you feel your body relax. Sit in silence feeling the vibrations resonate through you. After awhile, open your eyes and express with your art materials your representation of patience.

Part Three
Interfaith Appreciation

Interfaith appreciation began for me when I returned from an immersion course I took in Atlanta to learn more about Judaism and Islam in relationship to Christianity. I found myself sharing the experience with everyone who would listen. In particular, I spoke about community and about how each of the religions we experienced in the course focuses on creating and maintaining community in some form. Community provides strength, support, structure, and soul—all ingredients necessary for our walk with the Divine.

Our first exposure to community began on an early Monday with a Jewish *minyan.* In the wee hours of the morning, I witnessed a dozen or so older Jewish men chant and pray and sway and bow, sometimes in unison, but mostly not. The seemingly chaotic prayer service also appeared as a beautifully orchestrated, cooperative dance where no single person was in charge but rather all were glorifying God in a collaborative effort. This encounter was very different from my Catholic upbringing where the priest clearly led the mass with the expectation that we follow him.

> A *minyan* in Judaism refers to the quorum of ten male Jewish adults required for certain religious obligations. The term is also used in reference to public prayer.

At the minyan, there was no rabbi, but rather, as one of the gentlemen later explained to me during breakfast, "just a bunch of old Jewish guys holding the space in case someone is in mourning." He further explained that, in the Jewish tradition, when someone loses a loved one, the surviving family members mourn for a year. The minyan requires a quorum of ten men; so these dozen men have committed to attending the hour-long 6:15 a.m. service every weekday to ensure that those in need of mourning have a daily place of respite. They create and offer community.

Another insight I received from my new Jewish friend at breakfast was his observation about learning and understanding the Torah, the Jewish holy book. He said, "If something is obvious, you are not looking deeply enough." This statement summarizes the delight I witnessed our minyan hosts express in considering a phrase from the Torah. One host explained that God "speaks to us in the white spaces between the letters," implying that there is always much more to learn, much more of the Divine to be revealed.

Later, we learned about the Jewish prophetic teachings—Daniel, Amos, Jonah, Micah. I—and I'm sure many others—personally identify with the encounters these prophets described: they heard God's direct call and felt no choice but to respond accordingly, even in the face of extreme danger. Many times I have discovered a strength I did not know existed within me that allowed me to respond to God's lead.

I was introduced to the Muslim community through a dinner with hosts Hakim and Mara and also during a Friday afternoon at the Juma Masjid. Dinner with the young couple provided an opportunity to taste delicious, homemade Turkish food and learn about Turkish customs. They shared their experience of coming to the United States speaking no English, the differences between living in Turkey and Atlanta, how much they missed their Turkish community and family, and the difficulty they had making new friends in Atlanta. Mara also spoke about her prayer life and praying five times a day. She shared that since she desired so many material things, she needed to pray at least five times a day to ask for everything! I noticed the commonalities with other twenty-something young women who desire clothes, a beautiful home, and time with their husbands. These desires seem to cross all ethnicities.

My favorite experience was sitting on the floor with 1,000 Muslims at the Jumu'ah (Friday prayer). The imam's lecture, based on the story of Abraham and Isaac, was profound. He spoke about Ishmael and Isaac as representing the heart and head respectively, and that Abraham could not exist without both. I have probably heard priests and pastors speak to the Abraham and Isaac story dozens of times, typically described as "the Test." Instead, the imam approached the story from an esoteric perspective, noting the metaphoric internal death that results from cutting off part of yourself. He spoke about the pain resulting from living a divided life and the joy that results from integration, especially with God.

During the service, the imam quoted the Bible extensively and linked verses to what Muhammad shared through the Qur'an. I was astounded. In the hundreds of Christian church services I have attended, I had not once heard the Qur'an mentioned, let alone quoted. In a conversation with the imam after the service, he shared that Muslims consider Jesus, Moses, Muhammad, and others as prophets, someone who is selected by the Divine to receive a revelation. All prophets represent the same God, however the various prophets offered different rules of conduct during the times they lived. Muslims follow the rules of conduct laid out by Muhammad. Christians are encouraged to emulate the life Jesus led and the rules of conduct he provided as documented in the Bible.

One of the Six Articles of Faith in Islam requires belief in prophets as well as in God, angels, revealed books, the Day of Judgment, and Al-Qadr, a concept similar to the Christian idea of predestination—that God knows everything we have done and everything we will do even as we exercise free will. The revealed holy books in Islam include the Torah, Psalms, Gospels, and Qur'an. Jesus and the Gospels are part of the Islamic tradition and faith, so hearing these Christian concepts in a Muslim service is not unusual. Christians, on the other hand, believe that Jesus was more than a prophet; he was the Son of God. Christians don't recognize Muhammad as the next prophet sent by God to reveal God's word—thus, the unlikelihood of hearing the Qur'an included in a Christian service.

This interfaith primer provided me a sense of where these religions converge and diverge, and discovering their similarities was illuminating. Their comparable qualities discredit the prejudicial claims of my Catholic upbringing that Roman Catholic Christianity is the only path to salvation. As a youth I learned that anyone outside Catholicism was on the wrong course—whether they were Jewish, Muslim, or Protestant—and was condemned to a hellish afterlife. I was encouraged to pray for these lost souls so that they would invoke Christ as their savior through the Roman Catholic Church.

To my delight, I learned much from this introduction to the Abrahamic faiths. Each encourages experience of and alignment with a divine power within and beyond the self. Each allows its followers to be led by what resonates deeply inside them, and to become wholly themselves as individuals surrounded by community. Each faith has multiple names for this divine power and yet the essence of its strength is similar. Within each of us resides a still point that connects to something greater than our bodies, the essence of our being (God), another commonality in the Abrahamic religions.

Establishing The Ninety-Nine Names Peace Project

The Ninety-Nine Names Peace Project, which I began as a form of contemplative practice, can further interfaith appreciation by fostering a deeper connection with the Divine. In addition to painting the Ninety-Nine Names, writing essays and poems about my experience, and posting these creations to the Ninety-Nine Names website, I invite other artists and writers to participate.

My goal is to create an invitational experience on individual, community, and global levels. At the individual level, I invite anyone interested in creating sacred art and writings related to the Ninety-Nine Names to develop and submit their work. At the community level, I am forming salons: regular gatherings of people interested in literature, art, music, religion—creativity and spirituality of all sorts—that are held at someone's home. The idea of the salon came out of several personal passions: a desire to explore the Divine from an interfaith perspective, a calling to create art that reflects the qualities of the sacred, and a simple compulsion to make and share healthy cookies with good friends.

The salon is designed as a small community. We meet twice during the month, and each month we select a characteristic of God to explore (such as beauty, peace, mercy, power). The first gathering of the month focuses on exploring the selected trait (beauty, for example) through inspirational writings from various interfaith traditions, works of art from around the world, and other sources of poetry and prose, all focused on the concept of beauty. Participants are invited to bring excerpts from sources that speak to them, and during the evening we share these discoveries and engage in a facilitated, lively, and meaningful discussion of beauty.

For the next two weeks or so, participants are invited to reflect on the attribute of beauty and create their own art, writing, or music in response to it. During the second gathering in the month, we share our creative work with each other and talk about our experiences. Selected creations are then posted to the Ninety-Nine Names Peace Project website.

A global aspect of this project is possible through technology and social networking. In addition to displaying the creations submitted by participants, I host a blog focused on community, peace, and dialogue. Readers are responding to postings, and we are all learning about how we define community. Some of the questions I ask visitors to consider are:

- How do you define community (which could incorporate your village, city, country, nation, family, and/or extended network of friends throughout the world)?
- How and when do you communicate with other members of your community?
- How are decisions made regarding the welfare of the individuals and families in your community? Who makes those decisions?
- How are individuals represented and supported by your community?
- How does your community resolve disputes?
- How do you celebrate with other individuals or groups? What do you celebrate? How often?
- How do individuals share their gifts and talents with each other?
- How is your community diverse? Is this diversity celebrated?
- How does your community guide and care for its children? Its elders?
- What inspiration have you found by reaching out to those beyond your community?
- How do you create peace for yourself? Your family? Your community?
- How does your community engage in peacebuilding?

By sharing our experience of God through creative endeavors, we hope to identify the barriers that prevent us from engaging in community. Using expressive arts such as painting, drawing, writing poetry and prose, dance, movement, music, and drama, we celebrate cultural, ethnic, and religious diversity. Through social networking, we link individuals and communities, in person (through salons) and virtually (through the Internet). We hope to strengthen the connections that move us toward self-awareness, dialogue and, ultimately, peace: peace of mind, peaceful communities, and a peace-filled planet.

Creativity brings together disparate people in ways that political, religious, economic, and social dialogue cannot. I imagine one day in the near future experiencing the joy of artists and writers in community from all over the world, each working in unison on Restoration (Al-Muid) or Forgiveness (Al-Ghaffar) or Peace (As-Salam).

Selecting Insights from the Abrahamic Faiths

My process for choosing insights from the Abrahamic faiths includes a focus on selected lines from the *surahs* (chapters) in the Holy Qur'an and verses from the Old and New Testaments. I began by becoming familiar with the organization and thematic content of all three books, both in printed editions and from online sources. In addition to hardbound copies of each, I accessed online databases from the University of Michigan Library provided by the Online Book Initiative. The online databases offer simple searches, proximity searches, Boolean searches, citation searches, and the ability to browse both the Qur'an and the Revised Standard Version (RSV) of the Old Testament and New Testament.

I started by selecting surahs from the Qur'an, searching for lines that contained the specific name of God. For example, the portion selected for beauty contains the name Fashioner (of Beauty), as well as Creator, Maker, Mighty, and Wise: "He is Allah the Creator, the Maker, the Fashioner (of Beauty); His are the most excellent names; whatever is in the heavens and the earth declares His glory; and He is the Mighty, the Wise." Qur'an, 59.24

I also sought out verses that identified the characteristic of a name's particular theme. For example, the following verse speaks to the theme of creation: "What! do they not consider how Allah originates the creation, then reproduces it? Surely that is easy to Allah. Say: Travel in the earth and see how He makes the first creation, then Allah creates the latter creation; surely Allah has power over all things." Qur'an, 29.19–20

Next, I researched verses from the RSV Old Testament, focusing on poetry and songs. In both the RSV Old and New Testaments, I looked for verses that captured the characteristic of God for a particular theme and selected well-known verses over those that might be more obscure. When I found several verses that spoke to a single theme, I compared the multiple verses to the words of the corresponding surah and selected the verse that complemented the surah. For all three texts, I was interested in insights from the Abrahamic faiths that might offer inspiration to readers as part of their devotional practice. Out of the many options, I've selected those that speak to me. I invite you to do the same.

Participating in the
Ninety-Nine Names Peace Project

The Ninety-Nine Names Peace project invites people from all over the world to participate in our creative, peace-forming process—people from diverse religions, ethnicities, locations, ages, and creators of many art forms.

Artists, writers, poets, musicians, we invite you to *create* your artistic response to one of the Ninety-Nine Names of God in whatever medium you work, *connect* with fellow artists online, and tell us about yourself and your *community*.

Visitors, we invite you to view the *creations* contained on our website, *connect* with friends to share them, and consider how your *community* might become a more peaceful place.

Patrons, we invite you to support our work in this *creative* peace process, *connect* with participating artists, and consider what role your *community* plays in furthering peace.

To participate, visit us at **www.99NamesPeaceProject.com**

Recommended Readings

Al-Halveti, S. (1985). *The Most Beautiful Names.* Putney, VT: Threshold Books.

Ali, A. Y. (2007). Holy Qur'an. Bensenville, IL: Lushena Books.

Ali, M. M. (1991). Holy Qur'an. Ahmadiyya Anjuman Ishaat.

Assisi, St. F. and M. Starr (2007). *Saint Frances of Assisi: Devotions, Prayers, and Living Wisdom.* Louisville, CO: Sounds True, Inc.

Barks, C. (2004). *The Essential Rumi.* New York, NY: Harper One.

Cutsinger, J. (2003). *Not of This World: A Treasury of Christian Mysticism.* Bloomington, IN: World Wisdom.

De Caussade, J. (1981). *The Sacrament of the Present Moment.* New York, NY: HarperOne.

De Mello, A. (1985). *One Minute Wisdom.* New York, NY: DoubleDay.

Douglas-Klotz, N. (2003). *The Genesis Meditations: A Shared Practice of Peace for Christians, Jews, and Muslims.* Wheaton, IL: Quest Books, The Theosophical Publishing House.

Douglas-Klotz, N. (2005). *The Sufi Book of Life: 99 Pathways of the Heart for the Modern Dervish.* New York, NY: Penguin.

Finley, J. (2004). *Thomas Merton's Path to the Palace of Nowhere.* Louisville, CO: Sounds True, Inc.

Foster, R. (2005). *Devotional Classics.* New York, NY: HarperOne

Fox, M. (1983). *Meditations with Meister Eckhart.* Rochester, VT: Bear and Company.

Hafiz and D. Ladinsky (1999). *The Gift.* New York, NY: Penguin Compass.

Hafiz and D. Ladinsky (2006). *I Heard God Laughing: Poems of Hope and Joy.* New York, NY: Penguin.

Halifax, J. (2008). *Being With Dying: Cultivating Compassion and Fearlessness in the Presence of Death.* Boston, MA: Shambhala Publications, Inc.

Holt, B. P. (2005). *Thirsty For God: A Brief History of Christian Spirituality.* Minneapolis, MN: Augsburg Fortress Publishers.

Hughes, A. M. (2005). *Five Voices Five Faiths: An Interfaith Primer.* Lanham, MD: Cowley Publiscations.

Johnson, B. C. (2002). *Hearing God's Call: Ways of Discernment for Laity and Clergy.* Grand Rapids, MI: Wm. B. Eerdmans Publishing Company.

Johnson, B. C. (2009). *Beyond 9/11: Christians and Muslims Together.* BookSurge Publishing.

Khan, H. I. (1989). *The Art of Being and Becoming.* New Lebanon, NY: Omega Press.

Khan, P. V. I. (1999). *Awakening.* New York, NY: Penguin.

McGinn, B. (2004). *Early Christian Mystics: The Divine Vision of Spiritual Masters.* Chestnut Ridge, NY: The Crossroads Publishing Company.

McGinn, B. (2006). *The Essential Writings of Christian Mysticism.* New York, NY: Modern Library.

Merton, T. (2007). *New Seeds of Contemplation.* New York, NY: New Directions.

Revised Standard Version Bible, Second Catholic Edition (2009). Ft. Collins, CO: Ignatius Press.

Saint John of the Cross (2007). *Dark Night of the Soul.* Alachua, FL: Bridge-Logos Publishers.

Saint Teresa of Avila (2008). *Interior Castle.* Alachua, FL: Bridge-Logos Publishers.

Smith, H. (2009). *The World's Religions.* New York, NY: HarperOne.

Swan, L. (2001). *The Forgotten Desert Mothers.* New York, NY: Paulist Press.

The Catholic Comparative New Testament (2005). New York, NY: Oxford University Press.

Thompson, M. J. (2005). *Soul Feast: An Invitation to the Christian Spiritual Life.* Louisville, KY: Westminster John Knox Press.

CPSIA information can be obtained at www.ICGtesting.com
224213LV00001BA